BUILDING SKILLS FOR THE

TOEFL

Carol King and Nancy Stanley

TAPESCRIPT AND KEY
Second Edition

Nelson

Contents

Note on using the taped exercises:

The **Objectives, Directions and Example** for each **Listening Comprehension** exercise in **Section 1** of this book have not been recorded. They are printed clearly at the beginning of the exercises and should be studied carefully before starting the tape, which gives the exercise number only, followed immediately by the main part of the exercise.

However, the **Listening Comprehension** sections of **Practice Tests I and II** in **Section 5** of this book have been recorded in full, including **Directions and Examples**, in order to simulate the test situation as closely as possible.

Tapescript for Section 1 : Listening Comprehension

Part A : Similar Sentences

Exercises L—1 through L—2 have no script.

Exercise L—3
1 Calculators are cheaper now than they used to be.
2 Motorcycles are even more dangerous than bicycles.
3 Comedies get better television ratings than documentaries.
3 Electric tools cost more to maintain than hand tools.
4 Engineering courses are much more popular than liberal arts courses.
6 People who work generally have better incomes than retired people.
7 New cars have fewer breakdowns than older models.
8 Natural materials are often far more expensive than man-made products.
9 Walking fast uses up almost as many calories as running slowly.
10 Ordinary batteries don't last as long as alkaline batteries.

Exercise L—4
1 It takes less water to shower than to bathe.
2 Peter's almost as old as his cousin.
3 There are fewer motorcycles than bicycles on campus.
4 Children are playing more video games than ever before.
5 Soccer is still not as popular as tennis.
6 Sue has always gotten better grades than George.
7 Vanilla icecream outsells chocolate two to one.
8 Fred and Alice aren't as happy as they once were.
9 Betty's not making as much as she had expected.
10 Nevada is more sparsely populated than Arkansas.

Exercise L—5
1 Biology students usually take fewer math courses than business majors.
2 College basketball games are better attended than baseball games.
3 As a percentage of student enrollment, membership in social fraternities is less than it once was.
4 For their foreign language requirement, students are most likely to take French or Spanish.
5 Professor Thomas has had tenure longer than anyone else in the Psychology Department.
6 Recent scores suggest that today's high school students are not as well prepared as they once were.
7 Physical education courses, once a requirement, are more popular than any other elective.

1

8 Five years ago, the number of students applying for financial aid was dramatically lower than nowadays.
9 Undergraduates do not have as many library privileges as graduate students and faculty.
10 Thanks to a surge in private endowments, tuition this year will only cost as much as it did last year.

Exercise L–6
1 If I had Jim's build, I'd go out for the wrestling team.
2 If she'd gone to the rehearsals, she would've known her lines.
3 If they hadn't gone on vacation, their house wouldn't have been broken into.
4 If only she had the time, she'd be a volunteer at the hospital.
5 If I'd heard about your accident, I would have come immediately.
6 He would have stayed if he hadn't run out of cash.
7 If we had more time, we could do a better job.
8 If I were you, I'd be tickled to death.
9 Jack would be mad if he were here.
10 Unless I were well, I wouldn't be at school.
11 Had we left earlier, we wouldn't have missed the train.
12 If I were in your shoes, I'd audition for the marching band.
13 If Sylvia weren't so hot-tempered, she'd have more friends.
14 Had the invitation arrived in time, I wouldn't have missed the party.
15 If Pete weren't so selfish, he'd lend you the record.

Exercise L–7
1 We would've dropped by if we had thought you'd still be up.
2 If we'd known the zoo was closed, we could've gone to the museum.
3 If Mr. Smith thought he could get a better position, he'd quit.
4 We would've called a cab if Harold hadn't offered us a ride home.
5 If I had a quarter, I'd call my roommate.
6 Joan would probably move to Dallas if the cost of living there weren't so high.
7 If Thelma hadn't drunk so much coffee, she wouldn't have been so jumpy.
8 The soup would've been better if it had had less salt.
9 If I weren't exhausted, I'd love to go out for dinner.
10 If I were rich, I'd buy a sailboat.
11 John would do it if you asked him.
12 If it hadn't been for his brilliance, his drinking would have been regarded as a problem.
13 If it were the right time of year, they would be sowing.
14 If I had your experience, I'd apply for the job.
15 There would be no doubt about the result if John were making the decision.

Exercise L–8
1 I wouldn't be here unless I were invited.
2 If Tony were as talented as Bill it would be different.

3 If there had been more cooperation, the plan would've been adopted.
4 Had the two policemen not arrived, who knows what would have happened.
5 He would have a lot more friends if only he weren't so impolite.
6 They wouldn't have cooperated unless he had insisted.
7 If he had realized the probable consequences, he wouldn't have made the suggestion.
8 Of course he would've done it the way I did, if he had known how.
9 If you'd try it, you'd like it.
10 She would've told me if she had been there.
11 Had the idea occurred to him, he would've bought it.
12 It would be better if Mary were as tall as Elizabeth.
13 It would never have happened if John hadn't arrived.
14 If I were you, I'd reconsider the situation.
15 If he remains my friend, things will be different.

Exercise L—9
1 She didn't phone until after she'd gotten home.
2 I haven't run into Mike once since classes began.
3 Prior to her marriage, Edith lived in Texas.
4 Why don't you stop by when you're through shopping?
5 You'll feel better after a good night's sleep.
6 Until Mary leaves, we'd better not discuss it.
7 When they arrived, I was already in bed.
8 When the phone rang, I was half way out the door.
9 Since Harriet graduated, she's read nothing but fiction.
10 He played golf every weekend until he took up tennis.
11 After lunch, go straight to the laboratory.
12 How could you leave before the film was over?
13 Having completed one degree, how can you justify beginning another?
14 As soon as he stops talking, let's go get some coffee.
15 Having wrapped the package, she went to the post office.
16 After the war ended, he left his native England.
17 The girl opened her book and then made a pot of coffee.
18 We shouldn't have gone out until we'd finished our homework.
19 Their son was no trouble at all until he turned two.
20 George worked in the mail room until he was promoted to a secretarial position.
21 Since I began taking lessons, I have improved my game.
22 I'll meet you as soon as I've put the cake in the oven.
23 Having completed the requirements for the course, they were allowed to register.
24 You must return once he has given you the money.
25 Since the beginning of this month, I've gone to the movies five times.

Exercise L—10
1 Don't accept his offer until after we have talked.
2 Go to the post office when you are through with the typing.
3 Since I've had this job, I've met a lot of interesting people.

4 Amy didn't buy any new clothes until she'd lost 20 pounds.
5 I'll stay right here until I hear from you.
6 When the bell rang, we left.
7 Before you go for the job interview, get a haircut.
8 I asked her out because you stopped seeing her.
9 When they returned home, they found the mailman had been there.
10 I took this road because the policeman told me to.
11 You must do some stretching exercises before you attempt to run a mile.
12 Having failed to get into college, she joined the armed services.
13 Until they have enough money for a down payment, there's no point in looking at new houses.
14 As soon as it started to rain, the character of the game changed.
15 By the time the repairman arrived, Sam had already fixed the washer.
16 Until he graduated, Jack visited his parents every weekend.
17 May I borrow that novel when Donna finishes it?
18 Before you leave, talk to your father about your plans.
19 They didn't submit their application until the deadline had passed.
20 Once she improved her grades, Monica started reading more novels.
21 Once the alarm went off, I fell asleep.
22 As soon as it gets dark, come home.
23 By the time the bell rings, you must have completed the test.
24 Having decided on the menu, they went to the supermarket.
25 Hodge had escaped by the time Milton left the station.

Exercise L−11
1 His appearance was attributable to his diet.
2 Ultimately the late snows were responsible for the flooding.
3 The overripe fruit causes the animals to become intoxicated.
4 I was beginning to feel flabby so I resolved to begin an exercise program.
5 Malicious gossip often gives rise to damaging rumors.
6 She stopped dating him because he drank too much.
7 They found oil when they drilled in the southeastern corner of the property.
8 This type of skin rash occurs from overexposure to the sun.
9 The bird's nervousness is due to the demanding surveillance of its prospective mate.
10 They put extra locks on their apartment after several others in their neighborhood had been burglarized.
11 The disease can result in crippling paralysis or even death.
12 As a result of police enquiries, the man has been taken into custody.
13 It was not until he became friends with several of the board members that he was admitted to the club.
14 The phenomenon is produced by the Wankler Effect.
15 The whole problem was brought about by his undisciplined attitude.
16 *Gone with the Wind* became even more popular after it was made into a movie.
17 High cholesterol levels may result from certain diets.

18 Prolonged fasting eventually results in death.
19 He lost his job because of automation.
20 Failure to follow the instructions may produce drowsiness or nausea.

Exercise L–12

1 The last time I was there the waiter was very rude, so I haven't gone there again.
2 We stopped running because we were completely out of breath.
3 Due to the continuing prevalence of high interest rates, no immediate improvement in the situation can be expected.
4 After their neighbor's dog bit their youngest son, they filed a formal complaint with the police.
5 It was not until he had sold his car that he was able to pay for his operation.
6 Nervous collapse often results from a combination of overwork and poor health care.
7 Because of harsh frosts in Florida, the price of orange juice rose dramatically.
8 The sharply increased sales were produced by a vigorous advertising campaign.
9 There now seems to be no doubt that a number of diseases are at least partially attributable to smoking.
10 Using the wrong grade of gasoline will produce knocking in the engine.
11 As a result of the complaint, the authorities increased their vigilance.
12 A regular program of aerobic exercises may result in a stronger cardiovascular system.
13 Everybody rushed out of their houses when the earthquake started.
14 Adverse living conditions can give rise to physical adaptations.
15 After viewing all of the evidence, the judge decided there was a case against the defendant.
16 Lower temperatures in the vessel cause condensation.
17 A real recovery can only be brought about by sacrifice and hard work.
18 This type of warping occurs from dampness in the wood.
19 Unsupervised use of this substance may result in dependence.
20 Her chronic skin infections were responsible for her lack of self-confidence.

Exercise L–13

1 John must've gotten a raise.
2 I could've done that.
3 With training, Karen might have made it to the Olympics.
4 Ann ought to have realized Joe wouldn't do it.
5 I may have met him before.
6 The solution shouldn't have been that difficult to find.
7 Last night must not have been the first time that he roller-skated.
8 They couldn't have done it by themselves.
9 You should have explained it before we started.
10 Frankly, it's something Terry ought not even to have considered.
11 That is an idea Peter may not have thought of.

12 You must have been a beautiful baby!

13 I might have written earlier if I had had the time.

14 That trick of Bill's might not have worked anyway.

15 In other circumstances, they may not have won the game.

Exercise L-14

1 You should've reported the matter to the police.

2 I couldn't have carried that desk on my own.

3 It must have been the right color.

4 Of course, I could've come to meet you.

5 Jennifer shouldn't have ridden the horse so fast.

6 They ought to have acted like everyone else.

7 We might not have enjoyed the play.

8 She must've been very angry when she heard.

9 I ought not to have reminded him of his father's death.

10 Taking the job may have been the biggest mistake she ever made.

11 He might not have been so quick to agree if he had known all the details.

12 The price ought not to have mattered to the prince.

13 I could have finished it without your help.

14 They must've had first choice of the seats.

15 Tim could not have done that six months ago.

Exercise L-15, Sets A and B

1 The peel doesn't taste good. (pill)

2 That is my father's sheep. (ship)

3 The boy bit the dog on the nose. (beat)

4 Those heels are too high for me. (hills)

5 If you can't open the jar, try hitting the lid. (heating)

6 Sipping acid is dangerous. (seeping)

7 Her cheeks aren't looking too well. (chicks)

8 Those are big bins. (beans)

9 Did you see that lip? (leap)

10 He made a large bead. (bid)

Exercise L-16, Sets A and B

1 Tin exporters have complained about the situation. (ten)

2 The will was a source of bitter arguments among his heirs. (well)

3 There are a number of checks available. (chicks)

4 He felled his opponent with pleasure. (filled)

5 This is a big bill. (bell)

6 The den was too much for her. (din)

7 The writer pinned the opening paragraph in his study. (penned)

8 Your arm is in a bad shape but the wrist will be easy. (rest)

9 There are times when telling is really hard. (tilling)

10 Do you know what he bet? (bit)

Exercise L-17, Sets A and B

1 He spoke to the man. (men)

6

2 Does she have a ten? (tan)
3 He is said to be leaving. (sad)
4 That jam is expensive. (gem)
5 He is sending that dresser for me. (sanding)
6 Someone has bought the company I had. (head)
7 This pen is empty. (pan)
8 Who will bet next? (bat)
9 When work became too much, he slapped on his desk. (slept)
10 He is lending his airplane. (landing)

Exercise L–18, Sets A and B
1 Put your cup over here. (cap)
2 That's a very small hut. (hat)
3 There is a bag on the floor. (bug)
4 He was a brush salesman. (brash)
5 No lack affected their lives. (luck)
6 They caught the last bass. (bus)
7 There are many gnats out there. (nuts)
8 He realized it was too sudden. (to sadden)
9 That is an ugly mutt. (mat)
10 How did he get that lamp? (lump)

Exercise L–19, Sets A and B
1 His is a hat business. (hot)
2 That little cot looks comfortable. (cat)
3 He keeps his money in a sack. (sock)
4 He topped the former champion. (tapped)
5 There go the men; you can see their backs. (box)
6 He froze when he heard the clack. (clock)
7 It's unfortunate that girl is lost. (last)
8 People are safe here; it's just possessions that we lock. (lack)
9 Where are the caps? (cops)
10 You need a special knock to get in. (knack)

Exercise L–20, Sets A and B
1 This knot is very hard. (nut)
2 That cod is inedible. (cud)
3 I'll catch the bus if I hurry. (boss)
4 There's a short cot in the back. (cut)
5 He needs to change his lock. (luck)
6 She made a very good putt. (pot)
7 There was a dull exhibit at the museum. (doll)
8 Meet me beside the concrete dock. (duck)
9 She was in a lung ward. (long)
10 The boys rubbed the taxi. (robbed)

Exercise L–21, Sets A and B
1 The ball they bat is covered with horsehide. (bought)
2 They sought her in the library. (sat)

3 I must've left it at the <u>pawn</u> shop. (pan)
4 The <u>loss</u> was not known to me. (lass)
5 He was so <u>crass</u> that I refused to speak to him. (cross)
6 The interests of the committee <u>spawned</u> innumerable problems. (spanned)
7 What he showed us was a completely different <u>facet</u>. (faucet)
8 The baseball star came upon a young <u>fan</u> in the park. (fawn)
9 What was strange was that the animal was <u>clad</u>. (clawed)
10 I always prefer <u>brawn</u> to brains. (bran)

Exercise L–22, Sets A and B

1 You <u>sew</u> that jacket! (saw)
2 A <u>bought</u> man is no use to us. (boat)
3 You will be <u>cold</u> this afternoon. (called)
4 Dentists <u>gnaw</u> things that improve teeth. (know)
5 Do you like fish <u>raw</u>? (roe)
6 The <u>note</u> sounded strange. (naught)
7 They <u>wrought</u> the letters in iron. (wrote)
8 They were <u>owed</u> by the leader of the group. (awed)
9 This is a <u>law</u> office. (low)
10 We don't like the <u>coast</u>. (cost)

Exercise L–23, Sets A and B

1 He said it was true, <u>though</u> students were urged to attend. (the)
2 He gave a <u>bun</u> to the dog. (bone)
3 My sister left a <u>nut</u> on the table. (note)
4 "<u>Comb</u> whenever you like," said the hairdresser. (come)
5 The <u>cull</u> was small and of inferior quality. (coal)
6 His hobby is raising <u>homing</u> birds. (humming)
7 What you need is a good <u>robe</u>. (rub)
8 The goalie received a <u>puck</u> in the eye! (poke)
9 The ship had a <u>hull</u> that made it worthless. (hole)
10 The <u>boat</u> was too short to be of any use. (butt)

Exercise L–24, Sets A and B

1 He needed a large <u>board</u> for his aviary. (bird)
2 You'll find that in the <u>fur</u> section. (fore)
3 I'm worried about this <u>sore</u>. (. . . , sir)
4 At the coronation the king held an <u>herb</u> in his hand. (orb)
5 These tribes view cattle as money, and love to <u>herd</u> them. (hoard)
6 The councilman's <u>word</u> is always reliable. (ward)
7 <u>Warm</u> yourself in here. (worm)
8 <u>Store</u> the beans before they dry out. (stir)
9 She was sent to the barn to fetch the <u>curds</u>. (cords)
10 He kicked the <u>core</u> into the ditch. (cur)

Exercise L–25, Sets A and B

1 The <u>burst</u> threatened the entire neighborhood. (beast)
2 I gave my mother a glass <u>bird</u> for her birthday. (bead)

3 I never heed his instructions. (heard)
4 The sounds indicated that something was still lurking in the garden. (leaking)
5 They were asked to eliminate that particular weed. (word)
6 It was one of the most successful teams in the school's history. (terms)
7 The fur was more than we expected. (fee)
8 Watch out for the bees in the field. (burrs)
9 She washed the dirty sheet. (shirt)
10 This work has been very difficult. (week)

Exercise L–26, Sets A and B

1 The farmer was worried about his burn. (barn)
2 We ran into a curt driver on the way home. (cart)
3 Dart throwing is prohibited. (dirt)
4 These hearts are something such people must put up with. (hurts)
5 That's not my farm. (firm)
6 There was a filthy cur in the middle of the road. (car)
7 The bard was famous throughout the county. (bird)
8 Curve the bow like this and it will shoot better. (carve)
9 Can you see that fir? (far)
10 A great star greeted the birth of the baby. (stir)

Exercise L–27, Sets A and B

1 Sometimes it's good to pry. (pray)
2 His plate was unusual. (plight)
3 They just lay there without moving. (lie)
4 I'm surprised she doesn't get more pie from the bakery. (pay)
5 Stop! You don't need to sigh anymore. (say)
6 It's the way that I find confusing. ("why")
7 I prefer the white to leaving empty-handed. (wait)
8 He made an excellent try. (tray)
9 Flaying foxes greatly concerned the early settlers. (flying)
10 I think we should start with the hay field. (high)

Exercise L–28, Sets A and B

1 His mother bought him an expensive tie. (toy)
2 What is that soy for? (sigh)
3 She likes Roy very much. (rye)
4 The oil appeared to float on the sea. (isle)
5 The carpenter's vice sounded squeaky. (voice)
6 That foil is very sharp. (file)
7 It will take a lot of tiling to fix this roof. (toiling)
8 He could feel his bile rising in the heat. (boil)
9 He had several points and obviously enjoyed talking about them. (pints)
10 A young lady's pies can make all the difference. (poise)

Exercise L−29, Sets A and B
1 Hey! You stepped on my toy. (toe)
2 Are you going to boil that ball? (bowl)
3 The coal is in the garage. (coil)
4 They say that one's soul is the most important thing in farming. (soil)
5 His employer gave him twenty dollars for the extra toll. (toil)
6 The boy looked very handsome standing with his foil beside the house. (foal)
7 It buoyed us well so long as we stayed on the river. (bode)
8 A royal fell to the ground. (roll)
9 Is that a bow beside the target? (boy)
10 His loins were well-covered. (loans)

Exercise L−30, Sets A and B
1 There's a pin in the kitchen. (bin)
2 He brought a pear home. (bear)
3 His boast was a ridiculous one. (post)
4 This is an excellent pie. (buy)
5 What a cute little cub. (cup)
6 He took the yellow cab. (cap)
7 Put it in the big pen. (pig)
8 His pack was weighted down. (back)
9 It's one of the nicest peaches I've ever seen. (beaches)
10 Hand me that butter, please. (putter)

Exercise L−31, Sets A and B
1 Is all that tin really necessary? (din)
2 The deans meet every Saturday morning in the library. (teens)
3 How did you put that dent in your car? (tent)
4 Don't forget to include your new coat. (code)
5 The guide led us into the park. (let)
6 She never approved of any kind of fad. (fat)
7 The trunk obstructed our path. (drunk)
8 The train is in need of repair. (drain)
9 If possible, ride to my office in the country. (write)
10 We need two more carts. (cards)

Exercise L−32, Sets A and B
1 The gold eventually brought about his death. (cold)
2 He bought a new coat with the money. (goat)
3 He had just one girl. (curl)
4 I would put it in a class by itself. (glass)
5 What's wrong with your bag? (back)
6 Do they make clocks in Switzerland? (clogs)
7 The pretty green frock attracted the princess's attention. (frog)
8 Do you have any glue that might help us piece this together? (clue)
9 He was the owner of several docks. (dogs)
10 Any kind of gain will do. (cane)

Exercise L—33, Sets A and B
1 They objected to the buzzing. (busing)
2 He wanted his piece on a separate plate. (peas)
3 The price was what encouraged him. (prize)
4 I left a few pence on the table. (pens)
5 They wouldn't listen to her speech, but his they would. (hiss)
6 Did you loose the horse? (lose)
7 All I need is a zip. (sip)
8 The news was very frightening. (noose)
9 Her lies drove me away. (lice)
10 The ships brought a lot of spice to the country. (spies)

Exercise L—34, Sets A and B
1 He was wearing a jacket made of sheep skins. (cheap)
2 I told him not to make so much noise while he was shoeing. (chewing)
3 These new tiny chips can carry a surprising load. (ships)
4 I don't like that cheat. (sheet)
5 These shops are too expensive. (chops)
6 Would you please wash them while I'm out? (watch)
7 The fairy tale was all about three wishes. (witches)
8 Add some of that cherry sauce to the dessert. (sherry)
9 Please explain once more about the catch. (cash)
10 Can you match this for me? (mash)

Exercise L—35, Sets A and B
1 Did you hear that cheep? (jeep)
2 That man must be choking. (joking)
3 That is a most unusual chin. (gin)
4 Don't cut down the large trees. (larch)
5 It seemed like an age. (H)
6 The cheering of the crowd was very distracting. (jeering)
7 In the 18th century, he was a well-known designer of britches. (bridges)
8 I wonder if you could etch this for me? (edge)
9 Can you remove that jar mark from the table? (char)
10 It was the strangest lunge I'd ever seen. (lunch)

Exercise L—36, Sets A and B
1 How much did the fine come to? (vine)
2 I don't like the feel. (veal)
3 The veiled actress complained the whole time. (failed)
4 We'd like a room with a view of those flowers. (few)
5 She took her leaf. (leave)
6 He soon replaced the lost vat. (fat)
7 We bought a new fan. (van)
8 He was a member of a vast crowd. (fast)
9 Be careful with your fowls. (vowels)
10 If you add a "very", it changes the whole thing. (ferry)

11

Exercise L-37, Sets A and B

1 Was the vet any good? (bet)
2 You should only wear the best. (vest)
3 He insisted on removing the van. (ban)
4 How many volts will we need? (bolts)
5 Have we got enough boats to succeed? (votes)
6 The wooden vat was better than the aluminum one. (bat)
7 The problem was with the vowels. (bowels)
8 An unusual savor was left behind. (saber)
9 I don't like the way he jibed. (jived)
10 The women's libbers caused a good deal of trouble. (livers)

Exercise L-38, Sets A and B

1 It was the mouse that frightened her. (mouth)
2 In fact, of course, we have two thumbs. (sums)
3 This tree is very thick. (sick)
4 If you sink, you'll understand. (think)
5 Take the mountain pass. (path)
6 In my opinion, it's thin. (sin)
7 It was a very rare type of moth. (moss)
8 What I sought was illogical. (thought)
9 The math was rather difficult to grasp. (mass)
10 The norsemen were a constant threat. (northmen)

Exercise L-39, Sets A and B

1 The road was excessively long. (load)
2 The rice made me sick. (lice)
3 The light side was not difficult to identify. (right)
4 I didn't know what to do with my list. (wrist)
5 The rye did not help at all. (lie)
6 You must get rid of the lot. (rot)
7 If it's long, we'll replace it. (wrong)
8 Rust causes us more problems than anything else. (lust)
9 There is something wrong with that rung. (lung)
10 I'm afraid that loom is too small for the purpose. (room)

Exercise L-40, Sets A and B

1 Of course you mustn't fry it. (fly)
2 All you have to do is collect these papers. (correct)
3 The flight was awful. (fright)
4 It was a beautifully designed prow. (plow)
5 What an extraordinary crime it was. (climb)
6 If it glows, you'll know it's time. (grows)
7 The glass was a most unusual color. (grass)
8 It stuck in the animal's claw. (craw)
9 It's a brew they had never encountered before. (blue)
10 It was a flea market. (free)

12

Exercise L–41, Sets A and B

1 <u>Day</u> came finally. (they)
2 You must take one <u>side</u> or the other. (scythe)
3 That bull's not able to <u>breathe</u>. (breed)
4 There was something wrong with the <u>udder</u>. (other)
5 The problem was the <u>thighs</u>. (dyes)

Exercise L–42, Sets A and B

1 The <u>win</u> made all the difference. (wing)
2 The <u>bang</u> was intolerable. (ban)
3 It <u>rang</u> for hours. (ran)
4 One <u>run</u> was still not completed. (rung)
5 It's not a good idea to <u>sing</u>. (sin)

Exercise L–43, Sets A and B

1 It <u>stinks</u> right here. (stings)
2 There isn't time to have a <u>thing</u>. (think)
3 I didn't like the way he would <u>slink</u>. (sling)
4 Just watch them <u>sink</u>. (sing)
5 They were practicing in the <u>ring</u>. (rink)

Exercise L–44, Sets A and B

1 Here's the <u>wine</u> you asked for. (vine)
2 How much did you pay for that <u>veal</u>? (wheel)
3 He found it in the <u>west</u>. (vest)
4 We saw a lot of <u>whales</u> when we were on vacation. (vales)
5 They needed 500 <u>vipers</u> for the movie. (wipers)

Exercise L–45, Sets A and B

1 Put the <u>jam</u> on the kitchen table please. (yam)
2 The <u>joke</u> was difficult to see. (yolk)
3 He survived the <u>years</u> better than most. (jeers)
4 <u>Jet</u> planes are no longer new. (Yet)
5 I'll have the <u>yellow</u>, please. (jello)

[**Note:** In Exercises L–46 through L–50, Sets A and B, only the sentence marked with an asterisk (*) is on the tape.]

Exercise L–46, Sets A and B

1 * Put the pie on the window <u>sill</u> to cool.

> They <u>sell</u> soap.
> You must <u>seal</u> the envelope.
> His sister's name is <u>Sal</u>.

2 * There was an empty <u>seat</u> on the plane.

> Please <u>sit</u> down.
> They found a place and <u>sat</u> down.
> The gelatin <u>set</u> quickly.

3 * A <u>bat</u> suddenly flew out.

> He just couldn't hear the <u>beat</u>.
> I'll have a little <u>bit</u> of ham, please.
> He <u>bet</u> all his money.

4 * <u>Ten</u> soldiers died.

> There is a large market for <u>teen</u> magazines.
> He has some little <u>tin</u> soldiers.
> They got a good <u>tan</u>.

5 * The child has been <u>bad</u> tonight.

> There was a single <u>bead</u> of sweat on his forehead.
> The garden had a <u>bed</u> of roses.
> He made the highest <u>bid</u>.

6 * Don't <u>knit</u> your brow like that.

> The ballerina was wearing <u>net</u> stockings.
> He swatted the <u>gnat</u> with his hand.
> She always looks very <u>neat</u>.

7 * Motorists should <u>heed</u> fog warnings.

> He is the <u>head</u> of the faculty.
> He <u>hid</u> the money under a rock.
> She <u>had</u> a house and two cars.

8 * There was a welcome <u>mat</u> by the door.

> His <u>mitt</u> is made of leather.
> We <u>met</u> last year.
> That <u>meat</u> was tough as leather.

9 * He <u>led</u> them to safety.

> Put the <u>lid</u> back on the jar.
> Williams took over the <u>lead</u>.
> The <u>lad</u> is only ten years old.

10 * The plum still had the <u>pit</u> in it.

> The Eskimos roof their houses with <u>peat</u>.
> A toucan makes an unusual <u>pet</u>.
> There was a <u>pat</u> of butter with the bread.

Exercise L–47, Sets A and B

1 * How much is that ski <u>cap</u> in the window?

> Help yourself to a <u>cup</u> of coffee.
> The <u>cop</u> on the beat has a tough job.

14

2 * Try to suck on your straw quietly, please.

If you sock me again, I'll call the cops.
You can get a large sack of apples for two dollars.

3 * I can't get the knots out of my hair.

The gnats in the garden drive me crazy.
Do you sell unsalted nuts?

4 * He usually backs the winner.

I'll have a large box of chicken to go.
He says he's making big bucks in Hollywood.

5 * He removed his sodden clothes and took a hot bath.

The movie was meant to sadden the viewer.
His proposal was sudden, but she was ready to accept.

6 * I'm ready to change jobs; I feel stuck in a rut.

My younger brother has a pet rat.
If this is not refrigerated, it will rot.

7 * The shack was down by the river.

The shock of his death was awful.
Shuck that corn outside.

8 * He lost his wallet on the subway.

After his defeat, he no longer had his old lust for power.
You find out who the murderer is in the last chapter.

9 * Are you going to wear a hat to the wedding?

I'd prefer living in a hot climate.
They have a grass hut on a small island.

10 * After the match, both boxers had a few cuts and bruises.

We have enough cots so that everyone can stay overnight.
Don't let the cats out when you leave.

Exercise L–48, Sets A and B

1 * The roses will bud next month.

Her tardiness did not bode well for her success in the class.
It's too bad that he lost his job.
She was cast in the role of the bawd.

2 * It saddened him to pawn his father's watch.

The two old men made up one bad pun after another.
We had corn pone for the first time last year in Georgia.
You'll need a shallow baking pan for this recipe.

3 * The thief was caught in the parking lot.

Don't let the cat out of the bag.
She had to have stitches for the cut on her leg.
You'll need a heavy coat for Minneapolis.

4 * The children ate the whole cake.

You should call a removal company to haul off that rubbish.
Don't eat the hull; it will taste bitter.
Falstaff is a companion of the young prince Hal.

5 * Are you still mad at me?

They'll be late, their car is stuck in the mud.
"Maud" was a common name in the 19th century.
The railroads are still a significant mode of transport.

6 * There was a bust of Caesar in the museum.

The bast they used was poor in quality.
He likes to boast about his culinary skills.
The chairman of our committee bossed us around all day.

7 * Cal Tech has an outstanding academic reputation.

Many coal deposits were discovered last year.
I tried to call you, but your line was busy.
If hunters don't cull them, the seals shoot up in number.

8 * The boat sank because the wood had rotted.

The baseball bat broke when he hit the ball.
He killed the snake with the butt of his rifle.
Have you bought everything for the party?

9 * The ushers all wore fawn tuxedos.

They bought a fan when summer arrived.
Phone me when you get home.
Jack's parties are always fun.

10 * A frightened bear will maul campers.

"Mal" is a prefix implying a negative condition.
They were bothered by the mole hills in their back yard.
Our instructor told us to read the chapter and mull over what it said.

Exercise L—49, Sets A and B

1 * This is excellent bean soup.

It is illegal to burn trash in this part of the city.
Some things must be borne in mind always.
We are building a new barn.

2 * The wine is stored downstairs.

The knight's steed lay dead on the battlefield.
The poet stirred up some interest in literature when he visited the high school.
Please type the paragraphs that I have starred.

3 * El Paso is too far to go just for dinner.

They have a beautiful sofa covered with fur.
My lawyer's fee was outrageous.
There are four bases on a baseball diamond.

4 * The mean cur prevented the policeman from entering the lot.

The core of the problem is financial.
When are you going to trade in your old car?
The key provision is the one protecting minority rights.

5 * I need one more bead to finish this necklace.

Do you keep your bird in a cage?
The electrician bored a hole in the ceiling.
The male has a black and white barred tail.

6 * He'd do it even if she wouldn't.

The herd of cattle was driven across the state.
If this test is too hard for you, you will have to go to course 1.
The old miser guarded his hoard of gold.

7 * The jockey spurred the horse across the finish line.

The champ sparred with several young fighters every morning.
The plane flew at great speed.
The fern died after it had spored.

8 * We should reach port on Sunday.

The pert old lady decided to run for mayor.
The film star wanted a part in a Broadway play.
The farmers collected the peat to use as fuel.

9 * The child is crying because he's been stung by a <u>bee</u>.

I'll meet you at the hotel <u>bar</u> at six.
Can you help me get this <u>burr</u> out of my hair?
I'm not going to the party if that <u>bore</u> is going to be there.

10 * May I help you, <u>sir</u>?

The <u>Saar</u> is both a river and a state.
My throat is <u>sore</u> from all the cheering I did at the game.
Yes, I think I <u>see</u> what you're driving at.

Exercise L–50, Sets A and B

1 * Are you going to <u>buy</u> the group's latest album?

The rancher's prized possession was his <u>bay</u> colt.
The <u>boy</u> spent all of his free time playing electronic games.
He used his winnings to get a new <u>bow</u> and arrow.

2 * The students <u>say</u> the Pledge of Allegiance every morning.

Could you <u>sew</u> this button on for me?
Don't <u>sigh</u>. Let's look for a solution.
<u>Soy</u> goes well with many vegetable dishes.

3 * This project will <u>fail</u> unless everyone does his part.

A <u>foal</u> can walk almost immediately after birth.
He entered the room with his <u>foil</u> drawn.
You should <u>file</u> your nails before applying polish.

4 * The workman's <u>toil</u> was not fully appreciated by the landlord.

The <u>toll</u> for the turnpike has been raised by 25 percent.
We're missing a <u>tile</u> from our mahjong set.
The <u>tail</u> of the plane was moving from side to side.

5 * Phyllis lives in the next <u>row</u> of houses.

<u>Roy</u> was elected captain by his teammates.
I'd like <u>rye</u> and soda, please.
Sam's last <u>ray</u> of hope vanished when his opponent won Sam's home district.

6 * They say that a watched pot doesn't <u>boil</u>.

His job was to check the quality of each <u>bale</u> of cotton.
Help yourself to a <u>bowl</u> of soup.
Her <u>bile</u> rises when people criticize her son.

18

7 * The oldest living thing yet discovered is a pine <u>cone</u>.

Cane chairs have become popular again.
"Kine" was a common word in Shakespeare's time.
Speech writers often try to <u>coin</u> vivid phrases.

8 * The writer lived down a country <u>lane</u>.

The <u>lone</u> pine marked the end of the desert.
They planted a <u>line</u> of trees to stop the erosion.
I'd like two pounds of that pork <u>loin</u> please.

9 * He ran the <u>mile</u> in under 3 minutes, 50 seconds.

It can be dangerous when people <u>moil</u> around like this.
<u>Mail</u> this letter on your way home, please.
The <u>mole</u> used to be hunted for its skin.

10 * The painting showed several cottages nestled in a <u>vale</u>.

His <u>vile</u> language lost him the respect of his audience.
This would look nice in a <u>voile</u> with a flower pattern.
The <u>vole</u> is not a popular animal with farmers.

Exercise L–51 has no script.

Exercise L–52
1 His failure to get the promotion was a real blow to George.
2 It would take more than one day of rain to relieve this drought.
3 When I last saw him, Phil was the picture of health.
4 Karen tried to get out of the jam on her own, but couldn't and asked her mother for help.
5 It soon became clear that he was more than just a business associate.
6 Though king in name, he was unable to exercise any real power.
7 The congressman admitted that his tax returns were under investigation.
8 A hundred years ago, people were much more conscious of class distinctions.
9 The colored lights for the tree weren't working so Ralph's gone out to buy some more.
10 After his heroic rescue of the crew, he was showered with awards and honors.

Exercise L–53
1 *Beginning Russian* is only offered every other quarter.
2 The note was said to be counterfeit since some features of the handwriting were suspect.
3 Tell the kids it's time for supper.
4 When Bud got to the works, he found the whole place flooded.
5 Jean likes the material, but she thinks the check is rather loud.
6 The awarding of a degree is dependent on fulfillment of all departmental requirements.

7 You'd better be prepared for a hard examination.
8 The bridge club changed the whole pattern of her Wednesday afternoons.
9 Miller is certainly the hottest player on the team at the moment—and his smile shows it.
10 Those things are too dear for my pocketbook, Mrs. Brown.

Exercise L–54

1 On hearing the news, she flew out of the door.
2 The judge threatened to bar the press from the court.
3 Can you tell me what today's date is?
4 Pine Productions is a branch of Southern Lumber Incorporated.
5 You will need to season this with fine herbs.
6 The size of the packages that may be sent is limited by both weight and volume.
7 I'm afraid the press is outside, Senator, wanting to ask you some questions.
8 His violation was serious enough to require that he appear in court.
9 We were lucky enough to get a box just before the performance started.
10 Possibly the most distinctive call of them all is that of the cuckoo.

Exercise L–55

1 The institute director was responsible to a board of governors.
2 With that much play in the steering wheel, that car shouldn't be on the road.
3 Whatever happens, don't allow the engine to stall.
4 If you row down the river, you're sure to find somewhere along the bank to stop.
5 You're getting paid to do this; it's not all a game.
6 When the engine backfired, it sounded just like a rifle shot.
7 Economists forecast a world shortage of paper in the near future.
8 Men seem more likely than women to have a stroke.
9 The circumstances made it plain that the company would have to be liquidated.
10 Autos in San Francisco are required to yield to cable cars.

Exercise L–56

1 We can't match their skills, so we will have to beat them on enthusiasm and hard work.
2 That may not be what they're saying, but it's certainly what they mean.
3 Before Galileo, people did not believe the world was round.
4 They lost their account with a large cosmetic firm because the ads did not increase sales.
5 This agency is a government body and subject to government regulations.
6 You'll need to grease the pan well to prevent the meat sticking.
7 The spring dries up completely at this time of year.
8 The ball went right out of the park.

9 You'll have to move fast if you want to catch them.

10 The Russians beat the Americans into space by a matter of weeks.

Exercise L–57

1 There is a small chance that you may not get the house.

2 The owners of the building intend to file suit against the architect.

3 The secretary was asked to take charge of the arrangements for the meeting.

4 I'll bring one of my famous pound cakes the next time I visit.

5 As soon as they heard the siren sound the workers rushed from the factory.

6 Keep quiet or else they'll hear us.

7 The wave in his hair is entirely natural.

8 Of course the medium of radio was not available to politicians at the start of the century.

9 Many people complain that the rich countries are getting richer while the poor get poorer.

10 General Custer made his last stand at the Little Big Horn.

Exercises L–58 through L–62 have no script.

Exercise L–63

1 The boxer was in a daze after he was knocked down.

2 May I borrow 75 cents so I can buy this perfume?

3 The last king's reign was a very stormy one.

4 That little white lie got me in a lot of trouble.

5 He was in great pain after falling out of the window.

6 It's due to arrive early in the morning.

7 It was too painful to bare her skin to the rays of the sun.

8 The soles of the preacher's feet were burning after the march.

9 The metal desk they bought was a real steal.

10 The deer in the park are very sweet-tempered.

Exercise L–64

1 Such cosmetic operations are only for the vain.

2 There was a peal of thunder as they walked through the banana groves.

3 It was a long tale told by an old sea dog.

4 Prepare the dough before you cook the venison.

5 Treatment involves changing the type of blood cell, and is very expensive.

6 I have a fifty percent stake in this restaurant.

7 Stories of the black knights in armor are very famous.

8 The hunters combed the woods, but they found only a few hares.

9 A loud whine came from the cellar.

10 Let's meet under the beech at the edge of the woods.

Exercise L–65

1 I've heard all about those southern belles and their wonderful hospitality.

2 The boxer feinted with his left and surprised his opponent with a right to the jaw.
3 The actress took a bow when it was time to leave.
4 George was the only male working at the central post office.
5 Jane was very upset because she couldn't find the missing piece to complete the puzzle.
6 The site was ugly and a terrible place for the conference.
7 He didn't brake hard enough and smashed through the fence.
8 Sally and Steve rode up the river until their horses were tired.
9 She was looking at glassware while her mother was looking at skirts.
10 The doctor drank the contents of the mysterious phial.

Exercise L—66
1 In those times, only the great and wealthy had fireplaces in their homes.
2 They had to climb over a rather strange stile while walking through the fields.
3 People talked for years about the stuntman's last great feat.
4 Silvia sews all her clothing by hand sitting in her garden.
5 Her son's arrival took a weight off the old woman's mind.
6 The baby was borne away by its mother and we never saw it again.
7 Tickets for the county fair are expensive this year.
8 The priest had the power to perform the rite.
9 Her beau was very pleased with the way she had done her hair.
10 The Daytona 500 was only one of his victories.

Exercise L—67
1 Thelma got a lot of good buys at the annual white sale.
2 The airport was in the middle of a great plain.
3 The farmer's wife bought special hose to wear while working in the fields.
4 I bought this sail for very little money.
5 After adding a teaspoon of thyme, bake the casserole in the oven for 2 hours.
6 In the old days, bakers used to knead the dough with their hands.
7 If the truck driver hadn't given me a tow, I would've had to get there on foot.
8 The rich man's heir was a fresh-faced young man.
9 The elite corps of horsemen was the apple of the king's eye.
10 The fat woman would only wade in the shallow part of the lake.

Exercise L—68
1 My new dress has a fancy white collar.
2 The bucket of water was too heavy for the young girl to carry.
3 The escaped convicts were last sighted leaving the bus station.
4 In my American literature class last semester, we composed an essay every week.
5 My parents probably won't go, but we would still like to.
6 We had breakfast very late today so I'm not hungry yet.
7 I won't be able to to be present tomorrow because I have a dentist's appointment.

8 We followed the route taken by the stream.
9 The house that used to be in that place was my favorite in the neighborhood.
10 Have you seen Woody Allen's recent movie yet?

Exercise L–69
1 It was impossible for us to get tickets.
2 Santa Claus is said to travel by a reindeer-drawn sled.
3 The smallest boy always seems to be the object of the others' jokes.
4 Please bring in more logs for the fire.
5 The old man was too feeble to take his usual daily stroll.
6 Class ended early because the teacher's voice was croaky.
7 His hat was carried off by the wind while he was walking in the rain.
8 It's a pity to throw this away with the garbage.
9 Did you become acquainted with the new psychology professor at the party last night?
10 A solitary tree stood in the field after the horrible fire.

Exercise L–70
1 Things are not always what they first appear to be.
2 At what time do you close?
3 The people at Alice's office gave her a wedding shower.
4 The old people in the community were the thief's primary victims.
5 Cathy and Charlie traveled by air to Hawaii for their second honeymoon.
6 You should have a doctor look at that part of your foot.
7 My father says that live worms are the best lure to use for fishing.
8 There's a full gallon of ice cream in the freezer.
9 We will try not to be late.
10 There's a letter addressed to you on the hall table.

Exercise L–71
1 Sarah is better acquainted with Edward than I am.
2 The ocean proved to be too rough for swimming.
3 A large marine mammal was washed up on the shore.
4 You are wanted in the principal's office right away.
5 The technicians are finished with the initial stage of the experiment.
6 Have you ever gone to Canada?
7 She has a servant to help with the housework.
8 Look at that little insect carrying a bread crumb.
9 The tremendous strength of the champion gave him the confidence he needed to win the bout.
10 You should wear boots if you plan to walk through the tall grass beside the marsh.

Exercise L–72
1 My children are now fully mature.
2 The defendant's appeals for mercy were not listened to by the judge.
3 Can you tell me the fastest route for getting to the lake?

4 Were you acquainted with Mr. McGaffic before the meeting?
5 In the spring, this creek abounds with minnows and other small fish.
6 This workmanship is of very inferior quality.
7 The library is the principal building on campus.
8 I'd like a pair of those candlesticks, please.
9 Anthony has a very dry sense of humor, don't you think?
10 The rhythm of this song is good for dancing.

Part B: Short Conversations
Exercise L-73 has no script.

Exercise L-74
1 I don't understand what a root canal is.
2 Do you brush at least three times a day.
3 This might cost a lot, but in the long run you will see the benefits of doing it now.
4 How long have you had your office here?
5 Send the bill to my office, if you don't mind.
6 How long has it been since your last visit?
7 Tell me if you feel any pain.
8 My two front teeth are very sensitive to hot and cold.
9 I would rather feel the pain than have to have an anesthetic.
10 I'm afraid you're going to have to have this filling replaced.
11 I didn't know you could borrow records from the library.
12 Do you have your card with you?
13 How can I find out more about Roosevelt's childhood?
14 I'd like some help locating information on beekeeping.
15 This book is overdue. You'll have to pay a fine.
16 What time do you close during the week?
17 You should look that up in the subject card catalogue.
18 We have old newspapers on microfilm. Do you know how to work that machine?
19 May I have an application form for a library card?
20 I'm sorry, reference books cannot be checked out.

Exercise L-75
1 What courses have you completed in your major?
2 Which courses would you advise me to take in political science?
3 I'm having a lot of difficulty with Dr. Barrett's class.
4 I see you are developing a minor in Latin American studies.
5 Do you like the dormitory you're living in this term?
6 My roommate told me that all sophomores have to take art history. That's why I signed up for it.
7 You'll have to ask about a scholarship in the financial aid office.
8 Try to organize your time so that you can relax a little more on the weekends.
9 Do you have any more details about the junior-year-abroad program?
10 How many semesters of a foreign language are necessary for getting a teaching credential?

11 The speed limit on this stretch of highway is 45.
12 It's not an excuse, but I *am* a little late for work.
13 Our radar shows that you were going more than 15 miles faster than allowed.
14 Haven't you ever gone faster than the posted limit?
15 What's your hurry?
16 My speedometer must be broken.
17 You can pay your fine at city hall.
18 We were driving along talking and just didn't notice.
19 This license has expired.
20 I didn't realize that this road had a different limit than 71-north.

Exercise L–76

1 The sound has been very bad for about a week, but the picture is always clear.
2 We must have it fixed in time for the Superbowl.
3 What seems to be the problem?
4 Would you suggest a new antenna?
5 It's not worth fixing.
6 The baby was fiddling with the different buttons and knobs.
7 If you can't fix it, can you get us a good deal on a new set?
8 I'll have to take it back to my shop.
9 The problem's not in the TV, it's in the wiring.
10 How long have you had this set?
11 Please raise your hand when you're ready to have your work checked.
12 I didn't understand what you told us would be on the final exam.
13 I'm sorry my homework is late.
14 I won't have time to cover the entire unit in class, so please read it carefully at home.
15 Could you recommend some extra reading for me to do for my oral report?
16 The grades were so low that I had to curve them 10 points.
17 Your final exam will count as 40 percent of your semester's grade.
18 Will you give us a review session before the next test?
19 I expect this paper to be well documented and include a complete bibliography.
20 Please don't give us any homework tonight.

Exercise L–77

1 There are four emergency exits, two on either side of the plane.
2 We can help you arrange financing at the bank.
3 Do you want me to fill it up?
4 Please, watch your step as you get off the bus.
5 This little number can do over 120 miles per hour.
6 It looks like you need new spark plugs.
7 We'll be landing in about 20 minutes.
8 Do you have any questions about today's schedule?
9 Would you like a cocktail or a soft drink?
10 It's five hundred down and two hundred dollars a month.

11 Your back tire looks low.
12 The early inhabitants left these buildings after a long drought.
13 One previous owner, only drove it to church on Sundays.
14 I'm sorry sir, this is the no smoking section.
15 Can you please give me your tickets as you board the bus?
16 Check the oil?
17 We'll be stopping for lunch in about an hour.
18 This four-cylinder model is very economical.
19 You're not allowed to take photographs inside the building.
20 You should be able to make your four o'clock connecting flight.

Exercise L–78
 1 Let me help you with your luggage.
 2 Would you like to see that in your size?
 3 Please go to window number three for traveler's checks.
 4 Where to?
 5 I'm sorry. We're out of those right now, but we'll be getting some more in.
 6 Would you please endorse your check on the back?
 7 Your things will be ready tomorrow at six.
 8 The fare's on the meter.
 9 You can have it gift-wrapped on the third floor, next to the credit office.
10 I'm sorry; we can't cash second-party checks.
11 Your suit and vest will be ready on Tuesday.
12 Do you want me to wait for you? I'll have to keep the meter running.
13 Did you know your account is already overdrawn by a hundred and ten dollars?
14 Have you thought of a silk shirt with that type of jacket?
15 We can't guarantee our work on anything silk.
16 It'll cost you twenty dollars to go to the airport.
17 You'll earn 15 percent on this type of account, but there'll be a penalty for early withdrawal.
18 We can't guarantee the color in this sort of fabric.
19 We have a lovely assortment of cashmere sweaters.
20 Will this be cash or charge?

[**Note:** In Exercises L–79 through L–83, Sets A and B, only the sentence marked with an asterisk (*) is on the tape.]

Exercise L–79, Sets A and B
 1 * Joseph got a summer job as a fruit picker.

       If you and your roommate are going to bicker, you'll never get any studying done.
       I'm going to pickle these onions.
       Bigger schools usually have better-equipped facilities.

 2 * Don't grab. Everyone will get a fair share.

       What is that globe on your desk?
       It's such a drab day; maybe it's going to rain.
       Everything has been cleaned except for the drape at the back of the stage.

3 * Sam's muscles were too <u>sore</u> for him to swim another stroke.

All of the witnesses have <u>sworn</u> to tell the complete truth.
Jane and Sarah are both <u>sure</u> that Mark is coming to the party.
He had his head <u>shorn</u> for his part in the new play.

4 * They were both <u>finalists</u>, but neither was the winner.

This has to be the <u>finest</u> piece of pottery I've ever seen.
The increase of <u>violence</u> in the schools is a source of great concern.
If Chris had known the <u>violins</u> were on sale, he would have been the
first person in the store.

5 * The grass is covered with a <u>crust</u> of ice.

When they entered the house, they were hit by a <u>gust</u> of hot air.
My uncle's business ventures seem cursed with bad <u>luck</u>.
The taxi driver jumped out of his cab and <u>cussed</u> at the driver ahead.

6 * The <u>theme</u> of the play would have been interesting ten years ago.

I can't see a thing; the lights are too <u>dim</u>.
My parent's <u>deem</u> it advisable for me to go to college.
Why is everyone obsessed with being <u>thin</u>.

7 * This <u>gem</u> is worth a small fortune.

He'll have to be lucky to get out of this <u>jam</u>.
My grandfather can tell one fishing <u>yarn</u> after another.
There's not a <u>germ</u> of truth in this account.

8 * Don't <u>choose</u> a university without first looking at its academic
reputation.

These are very much like <u>shoes</u> which were in fashion fifty years ago.
A situation like that <u>shows</u> what a good congressman he is.
Who <u>chose</u> the music for the graduation program?

9 * I want <u>dual</u> controls on my next car.

The prisoners were forced to <u>toil</u> twelve hours a day.
He sat down and ordered a <u>tall</u> drink.
Do you have that garden <u>tool</u> I lent you last week?

10 * The <u>felon</u> was re-captured in the airport.

We don't want this problem to <u>balloon</u> into a crisis.
She has <u>flown</u> around the world more than twenty times.
The tourists reached Washington, D.C. when the cherry trees were
in <u>bloom</u>.

Exercise L–80, Sets A and B

1 * The film producers were unhappy with the <u>script</u>.

He didn't have the <u>spirit</u> to finish what he had started.
She won the race with her final <u>spurt</u>.
Jack and Diane <u>split</u> after being partners for twenty years.

2 * She could not control her <u>hunger</u>.

The teacher's <u>anger</u> was directed at the students who had cheated.
You can always find Chuck in <u>hangar</u> number seven.
When it's very hot, I <u>hanker</u> after the mint tea my mother used to make.

3 * Mine is the <u>silver</u> Cadillac in the corner.

I'd like one more <u>sliver</u> of that chocolate cake, please.
Few soldiers carry a <u>saber</u> nowadays.
The <u>savor</u> of fresh apple pies filled the house.

4 * The star witness's testimony was found to be <u>false</u>.

Can you give us a discount since there are several <u>flaws</u> in the body of this machine.
I'm going to run down to the store and get some more red <u>floss</u>.
Ken's all bruised because he <u>falls</u> off his skateboard all the time.

5 * I like to have a little <u>doze</u> in the afternoon.

Excuse me, are <u>those</u> your children over there beside my car?
<u>Though</u> I haven't asked her yet, I am planning to take Mary to the dance.
Dr. Kincaid prescribed a <u>dose</u> of cough syrup every morning and evening.

6 * She could tell from their <u>smiles</u> that Ted had won the race.

From what you've told me, I <u>surmise</u> that you were with Bob.
The desert people have learned to <u>survive</u> for long periods without rainfall.
The students were asked to find two <u>similes</u> in the poem.

7 * Susan was <u>crowned</u> queen of the festival.

When he went into the magic shop, he was greeted by a <u>crone</u>-like clerk.
How come you're digging up this <u>ground</u>?
By the end of August, my investment will have <u>grown</u> by more than 10 percent.

8 * I don't know about you, but I'm ready for a snooze.

  Nurses are often required to soothe frightened patients.
  A south wind usually means rain in these parts.
  Wearing a fancy suit like that without a tie is not traditional.

9 * Her father burst into a tirade when he saw her grades.

  The thief was caught because he tried to sell what he had stolen.
  Bill decided to go to vocational high school to learn a trade.
  Romanticism seems to be a common trait in their family.

10 * It is a great honor for me to introduce our guest speaker.

  Will the owner of the 1979 green Chevrolet, please move his car?
  He did not intend to injure the dog.
  You have an hour to complete this examination.

Exercise L–81, Sets A and B

1 * The recipe says to pare the apples and then cut them into quarters.

  With your head bare, you look cold in this freezing weather.
  If I peer into the darkened room, I can just make out the figure of a
  man.
  That was a great game: let's have a beer!

2 * The desk chair will swivel 360 degrees.

  Do not fold, spindle, or in any way mutilate this card.
  Phony realtors often find it easy to swindle gullible old people.
  When the bacon begins to sizzle, put the eggs in the pan.

3 * The cost of lumber has doubled in the last year.

  His blunder on unemployment statistics caused him to lose the
  election.
  Once they were again safe on their ship, the pirates divided the
  plunder.
  The passing thunder of the train was deafening under the bridge.

4 * Do you know where I put that string I bought last week?

  Be careful! This cleaning fluid will make your eyes sting.
  What kind of weapon was a sling?
  The trouble with living downtown is that you never hear birds sing in
  the morning.

5 * I can't quite picture the situation you're describing.

  I bought an earthenware pitcher on my last trip to the market.
  The vigor of his language made him an exceptional speaker.
  The vicar at the church down the street officiated at my sister's
  wedding.

6 * After two days in the jungle, his arms were a <u>mass</u> of insect bites.

Look at those sailors running the flag up the <u>mast</u>.
<u>Most</u> students come to class on exam day.
In the morning, it's pleasant to walk across the <u>moist</u> grass and smell the fresh morning air.

7 * If you do that, you will set a <u>precedent</u> that everyone will follow.

Can you help me think of a <u>present</u> to get Richard for his birthday?
His aristocratic <u>presence</u> made everyone take notice of him.
The <u>president</u> appeared on national television last night.

8 * My grandmother made me a beautiful <u>quilt</u> to take to college.

If you're going to <u>quit</u>, do it before the boss goes on vacation.
Silvia hasn't <u>quite</u> finished her essay so she can't go to the movies with us.
His doctors predict a <u>quick</u> recovery.

9 * There's always one <u>laggard</u> in every hiking party.

The wait was <u>longer</u> than I expected!
There is a <u>languor</u> about these summer afternoons that I find oppressive.
Cathy and Lynn are both in my French class, but the <u>latter</u> rarely attends.

10 * When it got dark, we pitched our tent beside a <u>creek</u>.

The policeman heard a <u>shriek</u> and entered the building to investigate.
In the film, Valentino played the role of an Arab <u>sheik</u>.
He had the <u>cheek</u> to tell me *he* could've done it better.

Exercise L−82, Sets A and B

1 * I don't think I'll ever learn this <u>waltz</u>.

Karen never goes for <u>walks</u> in the park.
Can you show me how this machine <u>works</u>?
You had better see a doctor about the <u>warts</u> on your hand.

2 * The <u>birth</u> of jazz is associated with New Orleans.

The pipes in our cabin <u>burst</u> when the temperature dropped to zero.
Stuntmen <u>flirt</u> with danger in many of their jobs.
Jim was <u>first</u> in his class in math and science.

3 * Listen to the <u>whine</u> of those racing cars.

Did you <u>find</u> the magazine you were looking for?
You have to <u>wind</u> the copper wire around the spool.
You plan sounds <u>fine</u> to me, but have you discussed it with Paul?

4 * <u>Beep</u> your horn when you arrive and I'll come right out.

If you just let us <u>peep</u> in, I'm sure we won't wake the baby.
All they ever do is <u>bleat</u> about how difficult their jobs are.
I'm trying to make a skirt with a <u>pleat</u> in the front and one in the back.

5 * He <u>thrust</u> to the front of the crowd and managed to get a good seat.

Representatives of the two warring parties signed a <u>truce</u> at eight o'clock this morning.
On days like this, people <u>thirst</u> for something cold and lemony.
He's the <u>truest</u> friend I've ever known.

6 * The two secretaries <u>split</u> the work equally between them.

The captain <u>spelled</u> the sentry for ten minutes so he could grab a bite to eat.
Ted <u>slipped</u> on the ice and sprained his ankle.
According to the children's story, Rip Van Winkle <u>slept</u> for a hundred years.

7 * He was <u>jarred</u> by the news of the plane crash.

A <u>cheer</u> went up from the crowd when the star of the film arrived.
It's easy to <u>jeer</u> at other people's efforts, but it's harder to do it yourself.
We'll have to go out to eat, this meat is <u>charred</u> to a crisp.

8 * The <u>lush</u> interiors were one thing I liked about the production.

Are you interested in having <u>lunch</u> with several people from the office next Friday?
This medicine will make you drowsy and may cause you to <u>lurch</u> from side to side.
Yesterday, I had to <u>rush</u> from place to place looking for all the things my boss wanted.

9 * The <u>expiration</u> date for entries in the competition is December 31.

When Carol was a child, her <u>aspiration</u> was to be the first woman president of her country.
Throughout this difficult experience, Mrs. Smith has been an <u>inspiration</u> to us all.
The patient's <u>respiration</u> pattern became irregular during the operation.

10 * <u>Mash</u> the potatoes until all of the lumps disappear.

The tennis <u>match</u> lasted just under two hours.
<u>Much</u> of this translation is too difficult for me.
I don't know why you like those romantic novels: they're just full of <u>mush</u>.

Exercise L–83, Sets A and B

1 * You're soaking wet; here, use this <u>towel</u>.

   The <u>bow</u> of the ship is not usually the most comfortable place to be.
   The <u>old</u> lady, who was a keen gardener, would wander around with a
   <u>trowel</u> in her hand.
   You must <u>vow</u> never to drink alcohol again.

2 * This suitcase is too heavy to <u>lug</u> around.

   For students, it is a <u>lark</u>, but the administration does not approve of
   their skipping classes.
   They threw another <u>log</u> on the fire.
   I think I may have run out of <u>luck</u>.

3 * I'd like another piece of <u>roast</u>.

   They <u>rode</u> past the house very slowly.
   Tim <u>wrote</u> his last book in less than a year.
   How long was your dog <u>lost</u>?

4 * <u>Goats</u> climb mountains with ease.

   Food <u>costs</u> are rising every month.
   Do you believe in <u>ghosts</u>?
   They bought a house near the <u>coast</u>

5 * You can get the <u>gist</u> of the article without reading the whole thing.

   His decisions are always <u>just</u>.
   The boat was capsized by a <u>gust</u> of wind.
   They hung the plants from a ceiling <u>joist</u>.

6 * The magician waved his magic <u>wand</u> and pulled a rabbit out of his
   hat.

   The <u>wind</u> from the north is bringing heavy rains.
   I'm worried about Alice, she's been so <u>wan</u> recently.
   Bill won't enter the race unless he's sure he can <u>win</u>.

7 * That's an elegant sweater. Did you <u>knit</u> it yourself?

   Sally's apartment was always very <u>neat</u> until she got that puppy.
   The <u>dean</u> of the faculty did not approve of granting tenure
   automatically to all professors with five years' seniority.
   Why are those students making such a <u>din</u>?

8 * You <u>flatter</u> me by wanting to see my work.

   New York is <u>farther</u> from here than I thought.
   Now that you've finally made up your mind, do not <u>falter</u>: talk to your
   advisor tomorrow.
   Washington is sometimes called the <u>father</u> of his country.

9 * How many people will your van <u>hold</u>?

Charles is showing off that <u>old</u> car he bought again.
Can you <u>hone</u> this knife for me before the meat is done?
They <u>own</u> a chain of drugstores.

10 * Kay is too <u>thin</u> to wear a strapless gown.

Some of the cheering audience banged <u>tin</u> pans together.
The kids <u>tear</u> up every magazine I bring home.
We were <u>there</u> for more than three hours, but we didn't see Allen.

Exercise L–84
1 They'll be landing in an hour or so.
2 You should see the mess the children made.
3 Pete'll do fine at the interview if he'll just relax.
4 Can I give you a lift?
5 Pour a little melted butter over the popcorn.
6 They're planning a winter cruise.
7 This store gives a discount to senior citizens.
8 You should have seen the look on her face when Bryan walked in the door.
9 You can take your pick of what's left.
10 Bill's come to expect good grades.

Exercise L–85
1 Could you speak a little louder?
2 Would you mind trading seats with me?
3 Would you like another cup of coffee?
4 Will you carry the luggage out to the car?
5 How about letting me buy you dinner?
6 Shall I take your order now?
7 Can I get you anything else?
8 How about lending me your car?
9 Do you want me to turn down the stereo?
10 Could you have my cleaning ready by five?

Exercise L–86
1 WOMAN: This box is as heavy as a ton of bricks. I can't imagine what I put in it.
   MAN: Shall I bring it downstairs for you?

QUESTION: What did the man offer to do?

2 MAN: You're never going to get the campfire started with such big pieces of kindling.
   WOMAN: You were a Boy Scout. Could you show me how to do it?

QUESTION: What did the woman want to learn?

3   MAN: This room has no ventilation, and I'm allergic to smoke.

WOMAN: Would you like me to put this out?

QUESTION: What did the woman volunteer to do?

4   MAN: The room was so warm and the lecture so boring that I almost fell asleep.

WOMAN: How about a cup of coffee?

QUESTION: What will these people probably do?

5   WOMAN: It's really raining hard. I'm going to get drenched going home.

MAN: Can I give you a lift?

QUESTION: What did the man offer the woman?

6   MAN: I've been home in bed all week. It's going to be tough catching up without notes.

WOMAN: Would you like to use mine?

QUESTION: What is the woman willing to do?

7   WOMAN: It's terribly hot in this little room.

MAN: I agree. Would you mind raising the window a bit more?

QUESTION: What did the man want?

8   MAN: It's really cold out tonight.

WOMAN: Sure is. My hands are practically numb. How about lighting the furnace?

QUESTION: What did the woman ask the man to do?

9   MAN: Do you think your car will be ready today?

WOMAN: I don't know. They had to order a part from the factory. Can you pick me up tomorrow if it isn't?

QUESTION: What did the woman want?

10   WOMAN: I'm so glad you were able to come to our housewarming celebration.

MAN: You really have a lovely place. Will you show me around?

QUESTION: What did the man want?

Exercise L–87

1   MAN: The doctor gave me a prescription for some antibiotics.

WOMAN: Why don't we stop at the pharmacy on the way to work.

QUESTION: What does the woman suggest?

2   WOMAN: The travel agent gave me some brochures on the
              Caribbean. Why don't we go there this year?
     MAN: Sounds great.

QUESTION: How did the man respond?

3   MAN: Your sister Pauline didn't recognize me at first.
     WOMAN: I'm not surprised. Why on earth don't you lose some
              weight?

QUESTION: What does the woman suggest the man do?

4   WOMAN: I sent the package over ten days ago and it still hasn't
              arrived.
     MAN: Maybe you should send the next one by air.

QUESTION: What does the man suggest?

5   MAN: It's already 9 and the next feature starts at a quarter past.
              But let's try to make it anyway.
     WOMAN: Why not? We've got nothing to lose.

QUESTION: What are these people going to do?

Exercise L–88 Sets A and B

1 WOMAN: I wanted to tell you how sorry I was to hear about your
            father.
   MAN: Thanks. I'll really miss him.

2 WOMAN: I hope you'll excuse me for coming to class late. My car
            broke down.
   MAN: I'm sorry, I couldn't hear you, there's too much noise in
            this room.

3 WOMAN: I'm ready to leave. Is there anything I can do for you before I
            go?
   MAN: I'd like to have the plants in the living room watered.

4 MAN: This is ridiculous. I've been waiting for my meal for more
            than half an hour.
   WOMAN: I know, but you see the restaurant is full and we're
            shorthanded today.

5 WOMAN: I don't seem to be able to do this problem. I'm following all
            the steps, but it doesn't work. I can't figure it out.
   MAN: Let me show you. That one gave me a lot of trouble too.

6 MAN: I have to take a beginning Spanish course next term. Do you
            know any of the professors in that department?
   WOMAN: Oh sure. Do you want someone who will make you work
            hard?

7 WOMAN: What's the best way to get to the anthropology museum?
   MAN: Do you mind going by subway?

8 MAN: I hope you understand. I'd really like to come, but we have
           to complete our inventory tonight.
   WOMAN: Of course, if it's not possible, it's not possible, but we'll miss
           you.

9 WOMAN: What a party! There are so many people here that I've been
           dying to meet.
   MAN: Yeah, too many. I can hardly move.

10 WOMAN: How are you coming on with your income tax form?
   MAN: Oh, okay. I've looked at it, and I guess I'll work on it after
           I come back from the park.

Exercise L–89, Sets A and B

1 MAN: I've been reading a terrific book. It's about the hardships
           which early explorers faced.
   WOMAN: I read that one, but I wasn't impressed.

2 MAN: That is the funniest story I know.
   WOMAN: That's not saying much.

3 MAN: Jeff can be very difficult to get along with, but he certainly
           accomplishes a lot.
   WOMAN: True enough, but that doesn't make up for his
           thoughtlessness.

4 WOMAN: I don't know what I'm going to wear to the party. All of my
           clothes look so old. It's too bad I don't have any money to
           get something new.
   MAN: Why don't you wear your black velvet dress?

5 MAN: You'll have to take this back to the accounting department,
           have it stamped, and bring it back here.
   WOMAN: That's at the end of the hall on the right, isn't it?

6 MAN: Please come back again as soon as you can. The spare
           bedroom is yours for the asking.
   WOMAN: Thank you very much. I had a wonderful time.

7 WOMAN: You know, I've heard that he inherited all of his money from
           his first wife and hasn't worked a day in his life.
   MAN: Oh come on. He was our mailman for more than ten years.

| 8 | MAN: | I'll be with you as soon as I give this man his change. |
| | WOMAN: | Don't worry about it. I'll have a look at your new books. |

| 9 | MAN: | You look absolutely exhausted! |
| | WOMAN: | I know. How do you manage to look so fresh and handsome after ten hours of work? |

| 10 | WOMAN: | Try to avoid route 11, they're making repairs along parts of it. |
| | MAN: | Okay, and you try to be here for our barbecue on Saturday. |

Exercise L—90, Sets A and B

| 1 | WOMAN: | Have you had a chance to talk to your landlord yet? |
| | MAN: | No, I don't know what I'm going to say. Do you think he'll try to evict me? |

| 2 | MAN: | This poster looks like it was made by a five-year-old child. |
| | WOMAN: | Well, if you can do better, do it yourself. |

| 3 | MAN: | I need some new jeans. |
| | WOMAN: | They're having a sale on them at Ogilvie's. |

| 4 | MAN: | You were hanging around the store on the night it was robbed, weren't you? |
| | WOMAN: | Me? It must have been someone who looked like me. |

| 5 | MAN: | How many times is this stereo going to need repairing? |
| | WOMAN: | I wonder if you shouldn't sell it? |

| 6 | MAN: | Have you had the brakes and tires checked? And do you have enough money? |
| | WOMAN: | I've taken care of everything, and I'm sure it's going to be a fabulous trip. |

| 7 | WOMAN: | That's the kind of car I've always wanted. |
| | MAN: | Here are the keys. Try it out. |

| 8 | WOMAN: | John is the best cross-country runner we've ever had at this school. |
| | MAN: | He might be good, but you should've seen me when I was his age. |

| 9 | MAN: | Do you have any books on running? |
| | WOMAN: | Of course. Are you an experienced runner or a beginner? |

| 10 | MAN: | Isn't that the anchor man from Channel 5 news? |
| | WOMAN: | No, that's the weatherman. |

Exercise L–91

1 WOMAN: There's a terrible odor of gas, but everything's turned off.
    MAN: Why don't you call Mr. Barker?

2 MAN: Remember, you said you'd help me with my homework for French class.
    WOMAN: All right. We'll work on it after I watch this program.

3 WOMAN: What time do we have to be at the gate?
    MAN: Go directly there. Passengers are already boarding.

4 MAN: There are plenty of sandwiches. Why don't you have another one?
    WOMAN: Thanks. I've already had enough.

5 WOMAN: It's so stuffy in here, I think I'm going to be sick.
    MAN: Let's go out in the lobby for a few minutes.

6 MAN: Wait one second while I put my boots on.
    WOMAN: Don't bother. The snow has melted and the streets are dry.

7 WOMAN: What time will you be through with work?
    MAN: Who knows? My boss usually finds something for me to do at the last minute.

8 WOMAN: I'm sorry you lost the race, Dan.
    MAN: That's nice of you to say.

9 MAN: The movie on channel 10 last night was great, wasn't it?
    WOMAN: Oh, I don't know.

10 WOMAN: Wouldn't you like to stay for dinner?
    MAN: I really can't.

Exercise L–92

1 WOMAN: I'm looking for paper towels, but I didn't see any under paper products.
    MAN: We're moving some things around. Paper towels are now in aisle number eight.

2 MAN: Has anyone told you what a fabulous suit that is?
    WOMAN: Why no. But I certainly appreciate your opinion.

3 WOMAN: Would it be all right if I use the station wagon this afternoon?
    MAN: Help yourself; the keys are on the table.

4 MAN: Fred's driving me crazy. I've heard him tell that same joke
           five times.
   WOMAN: Right. I thought it was funny the first time I heard it, but
           once is enough.

5 WOMAN: Thanks. I wish I could go with you, but I have to work on my
           term paper.
   MAN: Oh, come on. You can finish that this weekend.

6 MAN: We'd better hurry, the last train leaves in 15 minutes.
   WOMAN: Okay, let's call it quits for today.

7 WOMAN: Frank, why are those dirty pots and pans still on the table?
   MAN: I'm sorry, I forgot about them.

8 MAN: Let's get going. We should have left ten minutes ago.
   WOMAN: You're right, dear. I'll be ready as soon as I turn off the
           lights.

9 WOMAN: David really is some kind of mathematician!
   MAN: Is he ever!

10 MAN: I can't tell you how much I appreciate what you've done.
   WOMAN: Don't mention it. I had to go to Pittsburgh that weekend
           anyway.

Exercise L–93
1 WOMAN: I'm Gary's mother.
   MAN: Oh, are you visiting for the weekend?

2 MAN: There's a wonderful exhibit at the museum this week.
   WOMAN: Is that so? I'm really not into art myself.

3 WOMAN: Are you going to take that job the insurance company
           offered you?
   MAN: Oh, I'm not sure. There are so many advantages to my
           present job, but the insurance company is offering me a lot
           of money.

4 MAN: Do you have that article on private schools yet?
   WOMAN: The trouble is that I've had two other articles to write and
           the boss sent me out to cover that big fire.

5 MAN: It's too bad that Rob didn't come. He was supposed to bring
           some tropical music.
   WOMAN: Don't worry about it. Everyone's having a good time anyway.

6 MAN: Mmm—this pie is as good as my mother's.
   WOMAN: And I was hoping for something edible.

7 WOMAN: I'm a nervous wreck. I have to give an oral report in my art history class.

   MAN: Take it easy. You worked on that report for more than two weeks. I'm sure it will be very good.

8 WOMAN: I'd like to buy a turtleneck sweater.

   MAN: Are you looking for something in wool or synthetic fiber?

9 MAN: Can you tell me how to get from here to the stadium?

   WOMAN: I'd love to help you, but I'm a stranger here myself.

10 WOMAN: But everything is in our favor. We have financial and political backing as well as an excellent staff. We ought to go ahead with the plan.

   MAN: Well, I guess if you put it that way, you're probably right.

Exercise L–94

1 English teachers certainly have to carry around a lot of equipment.
2 I'm going to ask the florist to recommend something for my mother's birthday.
3 Being a politician is hard work.
4 Do you enjoy working as a guide at the White House?
5 The surgeon who performed my appendectomy was very skillful.
6 The newsstand attendant on this block does a thriving business.
7 You'd better talk to an accountant before filing your income tax return.
8 I wonder how many guests will be at the wedding?
9 Can you recommend a good electrician?
10 A language lab attendant is available if you run into any problems.

Exercise L–95

1 My sister is studying to be a lawyer.
2 I didn't know you worked as a gardener last summer.
3 It takes a lot of training to become a great chef.
4 All the guests seemed to have a wonderful time at your party.
5 Mr. Smith has been driving that bus for over twenty years.
6 Which dormitory are you living in this year?
7 The parking lot is convenient, but the attendant is not very helpful.
8 My brother goes to all the baseball games.
9 Do you know if Pete likes his job at the shoe store?
10 Ask the clerk. This pet store has everything you could possibly want.

Exercise L–96

1 How long have you had this job as airport security guard?
2 The price is stamped on the inside front cover.
3 You'll have to take your ticket to the immigration desk and have it stamped.
4 Do you have ten-dollar books of twenty-cent stamps?
5 I'm looking for a biography of Amelia Earhart.

40

6 You can send those flyers fourth class.
7 I'm sorry, you must book your flight two weeks in advance to get that discount.
8 I'd like to send this air mail, special delivery.
9 Arrival and departure times are posted on the large board at the end of this corridor.
10 Do you have anything on stamp-collecting for children?

Exercise L—97
1 That's the kind of bathing suit I was looking for.
2 I need two shrimp cocktails for the table by the pool.
3 You'll have to leave now; visiting hours are over.
4 It's another basket of fruit for someone in the maternity ward.
5 You'd better get out if you have a cramp in your leg.
6 Wait a second and I'll call the nurse.
7 There's something in this seafood that's making me ill.
8 Look, Dr. Melford has been building that sand castle with his son all day.
9 It takes much more patience than she's got to be a good waitress.
10 Give Mrs. Johnson her shots after every meal to calm her stomach.

Exercise L—98
1 You should use a good hairspray after you've had a wash and set.
2 We have nails in all sizes. What are you going to use them for?
3 I saw this fabric softener on TV so I thought I'd try it.
4 Now, you'll have to sit under the dryer for about twenty minutes.
5 It's 75 cents for the washer and a quarter for ten minutes in the dryer.
6 Will bleaching damage my hair?
7 This paint goes on very smoothly and will wash out with mild detergent and warm water.
8 Remove all the old varnish before you begin to re-paint your table.
9 I'd like my nails bright red if you have that color of polish.
10 Do you think these work clothes will get clean in this little machine?

Exercise L—99
1 This will have to be better on opening night.
2 You must pay your tuition when you register.
3 Yes, sir, all deposits are insured by the federal government.
4 The critics have panned this show, and yet it's sold out for weeks in advance.
5 The Golden Apple Award will be presented to the teacher who receives the most votes.
6 You will have to stand in line to make a deposit.
7 At this stage of the game, I think you should at least get to class on time.
8 As the curtain went up, the thieves were shown leaving the laboratory with the secret formula.
9 Please take your seats so that I may call the roll.
10 The interest on the money you borrowed for college has been raised to 8.5 percent.

Exercise L–100

1 Do you have any bags with you?
2 Watch the center, he's the superstar.
3 You'll find athlete's foot powder in aisle number 6 under pharmaceuticals.
4 Can I have an extra bag for this ice cream please?
5 The state university's women's volleyball team is staying with us this week.
6 I'll have one pound of chipped ham and four of those New York strip steaks.
7 Sorry, this facility is reserved for members of the basketball team from 8 to 10.
8 Check out time is 11 a.m.
9 Have you checked out this new body building equipment?
10 If you don't have more than 10 items, you can go through the express check-out line.

Part C: Mini-Talks and Longer Conversations

Exercise L–101

1 In lab tomorrow you will be examining rocks found in the Central Texas area, and you will be expected to turn in a completed worksheet before you leave.

2 Modern Western drama originated from medieval European plays on religious themes.

3 Heart disease kills thousands each year. Help protect your heart with a check-up.

4 You must bring a photo ID and your Dean's Course Card to gain admittance to the registration area.

5 The history of the earth is the story of the shaping of the continents and the ocean basins, and of climatic changes.

6 Some of you stopped me after our last class with questions about my grading system. I will base 50 percent of your grade on the three exams, and 50 percent on the final research paper.

7 One-plus dialing is still the cheapest way to call. And remember, our lower evening rates go into effect each week at 7 p.m., while our lowest rates start at 11.

8 This course has three required texts, all of which are available at the university bookstore.

9 Each student must have had a TB skin test within 10 days of the beginning of the semester. If you still have not had one, go by the Health Center as soon as possible.

10 The dirigible is a rigid or semi-rigid, gas-filled balloon that can be steered with propellers and movable fins.

Exercise L−102

1 I hope everyone is in the right room. My name is Professor Emerson and this is History 315, the United States from 1865 to the present day.

2 During the first four weeks of this semester, our focus will be on the art and architecture of ancient Egypt. The most famous examples from this period had religious significance to their creators.

3 Embryology is a fascinating science. We will follow the development of an animal from its beginning as a fertilized ovum until it is hatched or born.

4 In this lab course we will conduct experiments that apply the principles of electron movement that have been covered in the lectures. You will be expected to keep a notebook containing your results.

5 Our culture has thus far produced only one writer whose work is significant enough to warrant an entire course. We will read as much of William Shakespeare's work as possible, but can only scratch the surface.

Exercise L−103

1 Welcome to freshman orientation. This morning's program should answer some of your questions about how to register for classes.

2 As director of the student health center, I'd like to tell you a little bit about the services that will be available to you while you're a student at the university.

3 Before you leave, I want to remind you of tomorrow's field trip to the Whitehead Art Museum. Although the handout lists the artists we'll be seeing, I need to give you some details about the schedule we'll follow.

4 Your registration packet contains your Dean's course card. Fill it out before you see your advisor, but use a pencil so it will be easy for the advisor to make any necessary changes.

5 The staff of the International Office is here to assist you in every way possible. We can help you with immigration problems, financial problems, and even personal problems.

6 Mrs. Alice Thompson is Director of the Measurement and Evaluation Office. She is going to talk to you about the math and English placement tests that each of you must take prior to registration.

7 Finished with your studying and no place to go? Come to the Student Union. You should consider it your home away from home. We have a variety of activities going on every day.

8 On behalf of the entire staff and management, I want to welcome you to the University Student Art Gallery. This month's exhibit contains a wide variety of three-dimensional art objects and goes far beyond mere sculpture.

9 Facing a difficult problem? Need some advice? The doors are always open at the University Counseling Center. Just call 472-HELP for an appointment with a member of our trained staff of psychologists.

10 We're pleased to have such a large turn-out for this year's first meeting of the University Sailing Club. The officers have had several planning sessions, and we'd like to share some of our ideas.

Exercise L–104
1 Where are most deserts found?
2 What is erosion?
3 How are all electromagnetic waves alike?
4 What happens to the diaphragm when a person breathes?
5 How do bees find their way home?
6 Why was Charles Dickens' writing important?
7 How is a delta formed?
8 Why were Thomas Hart Benton's paintings considered revolutionary?
9 What is the speaker's opinion of Homer?
10 What is one advantage of dehydrated food?

Exercise L–105 has no script.

Exercise L–106
[Portion 1:]
Welcome to freshman orientation. The faculty and staff hope that today's program will answer some of your questions about the university. We're going to begin with information concerning the two-day registration period that begins tomorrow.

[Portion 2:]
If you follow the basic steps I'm going to outline for you, even your first registration can be hassle-free.

[Portion 3:]
By now, you should have received the orientation packet in the mail. If not, please pick one up as you leave the auditorium.

[Portion 4:]
The packet contains a schedule of the times and locations of the required placement tests in math and English. Taking these tests is the first step in registration.

[Portion 5:]
The next step is a visit to the Academic Center where you pick up a course schedule and your registration materials. Be sure to take a photo ID and your letter of acceptance.

[Portion 6:]
Then, proceed to your department to have your Course Request Card approved and signed by a faculty advisor. Registration itself takes place at the Special Events Center.

[Portion 7:]
Don't forget to bring your checkbook or cash to the Center as you are required to pay all fees at the time you turn in your registration materials.

[Portion 8:]
Before introducing our next speaker, I'd like to thank you for your attention and wish you good luck this semester.

Exercise L–107

[Portion 1:]
People all over the world know what cowboys are. They are the most famous symbols of the Days of the Old West. This well-known period of American history lasted only fifty years and was gone by the end of the nineteenth century. Few people realize how short it really was, or why it ended. One reason it came to such an abrupt end was the invention of a new kind of fencing material called barbed wire.

[Portion 2:]
Who invented barbed wire? That's not an easy question to answer. History books give Alphonso Dobb credit because he took out the first patent on it in 1867. But some historians don't believe he really invented it. They say that a Swiss-born Texan named John Gillinger came up with the idea first.

[Portion 3:]
Gillinger had a lot of trouble with his garden. Cattle broke through his fences and trampled it; children climbed over the fences and stole fruit off his trees. So he set out to build a fence neither of them could ignore. He took two strands of smooth wire and twisted them together. Every few inches he inserted between them dangerous barbs made out of sharp pieces of iron and small bits of broken glass.

[Portion 4:]
Gillinger's barbed wire fence quickly earned a wide-spread reputation in

Texas, and eventually all across the West. Before the turn of the century over four hundred different designs for barbed wire were developed and marketed. But Gillinger's basic idea has yet to be improved on.

Exercise L–108

Women are more involved in sports than they used to be. And, they are frequently beating their male counterparts in events like marathon running and long-distance swimming, events that require stamina as well as strength.

    1 **In what kinds of events do women outperform men?**
    2 **According to the speaker, how many women are involved in sports?**
    3 **In the speaker's opinion, why are men better long-distance runners?**
    4 **In what kinds of races are women more likely to beat men?**

What gives women their greater endurance? The answer seems to lie in the female physiology. Endurance depends not on muscle, but on fat. Although a man has a higher percentage of muscle tissue than a woman, the woman has relatively more fat. On the average, 25 percent of her body weight is fat, compared with only 15 percent in men.

    5 **What percentage of a man's weight does fat account for?**
    6 **According to the speaker, what gives men greater endurance?**
    7 **In what way is a man's physiology different from a woman's?**
    8 **In the speaker's opinion, what is the real source of an athlete's stamina?**

The difference gives women at least two advantages in endurance events. Because fat is significantly lighter than muscle, a woman has far less weight to carry around than a man of the same age and height. The second advantage, however, is more important. Muscles need fuel to function. After the body uses up its ready supply of fuel, it must switch to fat. With their greater proportion of fat, women simply have more fuel available. Their bodies are also more accustomed to utilizing fat and do it more efficiently.

    9 **Why are women at a disadvantage, according to the speaker?**
   10 **What does the speaker say is the basic physiological difference between a man and woman of the same age and height?**
   11 **What source of energy does the human body utilize first in marathon events?**
   12 **Why are men better able to use their muscles for strength?**

Tapescript for Section 5:
Practice Tests I and II

Before you begin either of these tests, remove the answer sheets from the back of the book containing the Tapescript and Answer Key.

When you take the actual TOEFL, you will have only a pencil, an eraser, your watch and the test book and answer sheet on your desk. You will not be allowed to take any dictionaries or other books into the test room.

You must not write in the test book; mark all your answers clearly on the answer sheet provided by completely blackening the oval which corresponds to the answer you have chosen. If you wish to change an answer, completely erase your first answer and make your new answer.

Answer every question; mark your best guess if you are not sure of an answer.

Practice Test I

Print your name in the box provided at the top of the answer sheet. Print your family name, (or surname), first. Then print your first name. You will now have 15 seconds to do this.

[15 second pause]

Now open your book at Practice Test I and listen to the directions for the Listening Comprehension Section:

Practice Test I: Section 1
Listening Comprehension

In this section of the test, you will have an opportunity to demonstrate your ability to understand spoken English. There are three parts to this section, with special directions for each part.

Part A

Directions: For each problem in Part A, you will hear a short statement. The statements will be spoken just one time. They will not be written out for you, and you must listen carefully in order to understand what the speaker says.

When you hear a statement, read the four sentences in your test book and decide which one is closest in meaning to the statement you have heard. Then, on your answer sheet, find the number of the problem and mark your answer.

Listen to the following example:

You will hear:
If you had arrived a day earlier, you would have met the ambassador and his family.

You will read: (A) The ambassador enjoyed meeting you and your family.
(B) You missed the ambassador by a day.
(C) Earlier in the day, the ambassador met with his family.
(D) Yesterday's meeting with the ambassador was cancelled.

Sentence (B), "You missed the ambassador by a day," is closest in meaning to the sentence, "If you had arrived a day earlier, you would have met the ambassador and his family." Therefore, you should choose answer (B).

Listen to the next example:

You will hear:
Dave volunteered to bring his station wagon so that everyone could go at the same time.

You will read: (A) Dave will be the only person driving this time.
(B) Dave will call the station.
(C) The party left from the same station as last time.
(D) Dave is a volunteer fireman at our local station.

Sentence (A), "Dave will be the only person driving this time," means most nearly the same as the statement "Dave volunteered to bring his station wagon so that everyone could go at the same time." Therefore, you should choose answer (A).

Now let us begin Part A with question number one:

1 My next door neighbor's son is always getting into trouble.
2 When she got back from the South, Susan had her car washed.
3 If Jack had only had more money for TV spots, he probably would've won the election.
4 There's food on these plates; the children must've already eaten.
5 Betty did not receive credit for the course because she hadn't paid the lab fee.
6 If I were in his shoes, I'd be worried about the expense.
7 His team finished next to last.
8 She was too surprised to speak.
9 Whether the library is open this weekend or not, you have to finish your term paper before Monday.
10 The fact that Fred is a highly qualified medical doctor doesn't mean that he can advise you about psychological questions.
11 Paul skipped all of his classes yesterday and today, but he must take the final exams tomorrow.
12 She let herself in for the hardships she's facing now.
13 In order to meet the deadline for the project, Francis and Bill had their parents help them out.
14 She's sure he tried to hurt her feelings on purpose.
15 The interest on the money you borrowed for your tuition has been raised to 10.5 percent.

16 Every day Ben intends to get to the office early, but his bus is almost always late.
17 I've driven around this block five times, but I still can't locate Bill's new house.
18 Dr. Elkins' lecture was cut short by a fire drill.
19 Amy has been sipping on that same soda for the last half hour.
20 Carl became very ill at ease during his interview with the recruiter.

This is the end of Part A.
Now listen to the directions for Part B, as they are read to you:

Part B

<u>Directions</u>: In Part B you will hear fifteen short conversations between two speakers. At the end of each conversation, a third voice will ask a question about what was said. The question will be <u>spoken</u> just one time. After you hear a conversation and the question about it, read the four possible answers and decide which one would be the best answer to the question you have heard. Then, on your answer sheet, find the number of the problem and mark your answer.

Listen to the following example:

   You will hear:
       MAN: Jim's been so difficult since he gave up smoking!
    WOMAN: Yes, but it'll make a new man of him in the long run.
   QUESTION: What does the woman mean?

   You will read: (A) Jim is beginning to act like an adult.
               (B) Jim will eventually benefit from giving up cigarettes.
               (C) Jim has been having a hard time since he started smoking.
               (D) Jim is becoming a better long-distance runner.

From the conversation we know that Jim has recently stopped smoking, and that the woman feels that this will eventually help him. The best answer, then, is (B), "Jim will eventually benefit from giving up cigarettes." Therefore, you should choose answer (B).

Now let us begin Part B with question number 21:

21   JANE: I'll go change my clothes as soon as I finish typing this essay.
          MAN: Okay, Jane. Then we'll take my car and go out for a meal.

   QUESTION: What is Jane going to do now?

22   MAN: George is already more than an hour late. Do you think he changed his mind about joining us?
     WOMAN: That's hard for me to say.

   QUESTION: What conclusion can be drawn from the woman's statement?

23	WOMAN:	The attitude of the hotel staff here is incredible.
	MAN:	Right. It's high time they got rid of half of them if you ask me.
	QUESTION:	What can be concluded from the conversation?

23   WOMAN: The attitude of the hotel staff here is incredible.
      MAN: Right. It's high time they got rid of half of them if you ask me.

      QUESTION: What can be concluded from the conversation?

24   MAN: Do you have Blodsky's latest collection of plays?
      WOMAN: Yes, we do, but I'm afraid it's checked out at the moment.

      QUESTION: Where did this conversation take place?

25   WOMAN: You know, I've tried to even up the legs of my typewriter table, but I just don't seem to be able to get them right.
      MAN: If I were you, I'd get Mrs. Roberts to come and do them.

      QUESTION: What does Mrs. Roberts do?

26   MAN: Do you mind if I open this window?
      WOMAN: As a matter of fact, I'm feeling a bit chilly.

      QUESTION: What does the woman want the man to do?

27   WOMAN: I suppose you've heard that Phil's moving up in the world since he went to Los Angeles.
      MAN: Yes, Judy told me that he's no longer working for his father.

      QUESTION: What can be said about Phil?

28   MAN: This cake is delicious. Where did you buy it?
      WOMAN: It's my own creation. It's something like my mother's chocolate cake.

      QUESTION: Who made the cake?

29   WOMAN: The problem is that I don't get paid until tomorrow, but I must register for Dr. Johnson's class. Could you hold a place for me until tomorrow?
      MAN: I'm sure you know that we are not permitted to reserve spaces in a class without full payment or a note from the professor. You'll have to wait and take your chances.

      QUESTION: What did the man mean?

30   WOMAN: Ron, could I borrow fifty dollars? I'll be happy to pay you back, with interest, at the end of next week.
      RON: You have a lot of nerve asking me to lend you money after acting as if you didn't even know me at the reception last night.

      QUESTION: How did Ron respond?

31	MAN:	I used to love this restaurant. For years, they had the best Italian food in town.
	WOMAN:	I agree. It was one of my favorites too until they redecorated and hired a new chef.
	QUESTION:	What did the man and woman say about the restaurant?

32	MAN:	Why don't we call a babysitter, get dressed up, and go out on the town this evening?
	WOMAN:	Darling, that sounds fabulous, but can we afford it?
	QUESTION:	What does the man want to do?

33	MAN:	Here's your taxi, Mr. Taylor. Sorry you won't be with us for the trip to the ruins and the farewell banquet.
	MR. TAYLOR:	I hate missing the end of the tour, but my partner insists I be back for the board meeting on Monday morning.
	QUESTION:	Why is Mr. Taylor leaving early?

34	MAN:	I need some new clothes. None of my blue jeans fit, and I can't even button my suit jacket.
	WOMAN:	Maybe you should first start counting your calories and then worry about your wardrobe.
	QUESTION:	What did the woman suggest?

35	MAN:	Tell me about the best-seller you bought this morning.
	WOMAN:	It's great. It's full of political intrigue and describes the romances of different members of a very wealthy Washington family.
	QUESTION:	What is the woman talking about?

This is the end of Part B.

Now look at the directions for Part C, as they are read to you:

Part C

Directions: In this part of the test, you will hear several short talks and/or conversations. After each talk or conversation, you will be asked some questions. The talks and questions will be spoken just one time. They will not be written out for you, so you will have to listen carefully in order to understand and remember what the speaker says.

When you hear a question, read the four possible answers in your test book and decide which one would be the best answer to the question you have heard. Then, on your answer sheet, find the number of the problem and fill in (blacken) the space that corresponds to the letter of the answer you have chosen.

Listen to this sample talk:

The origin of the modern American custom of sending greeting cards for almost any occasion can be traced back to Europe in the 15th century when people sent inscribed prints to friends and relatives to mark the beginning of the New Year.

In the mid-19th century, John Calcott Horslev, an Englishman, designed what is considered to be the first Christmas card. Shortly thereafter, Louis Prang of Boston, often called the father of the American Christmas card, began issuing sets of cards with an appropriate message for the Christmas season, and by 1880 he was offering prizes for attractive greeting card designs.

Until this century, Americans imported a large percentage of their greeting cards from Europe, but about 75 or so years ago, this situation changed and now the United States produces cards in great quantity and variety.

Today, Americans send cards to friends and relatives for birthdays, for annual festivities such as Christmas and Easter, as well as simply as an expression of good will.

Now listen to the first question on the sample talk:

You will hear:
When did Americans probably begin to send Christmas cards?

You will read: (A) In the 15th century.
(B) In the 19th century.
(C) In this century.
(D) About 1910.

The best answer to the question, "When did Americans probably begin to send Christmas cards?" is (B), "In the 19th century." Therefore, you should choose answer (B).

Now listen to the second question on the sample talk:

You will hear:
Which of the following most accurately describes why Americans send greeting cards?

You will read: (A) To celebrate birthdays.
(B) To acknowledge holidays.
(C) To commemorate birthdays, Christmas and Easter.
(D) To wish others well on almost any occasion.

The best answer to the question "Which of the following most accurately describes why Americans send greeting cards?" is (D), "To wish others well on almost any occasion." Therefore, you should choose answer (D).

Questions 36 through 41 refer to the following conversation:

STUDENT: Dr. Taylor, I'd like to talk to you about working as your assistant next quarter.
DR. TAYLOR: Fine, please come in and sit down. Have you read the list of

requirements for assistants in the English Department?

STUDENT: Yes sir. I'm an English major. I'm a junior now, but I'll be a senior next term and my grade point average is 3.3.

DR. TAYLOR: That's fine then. Now why don't you tell me why you'd like to be *my* assistant.

STUDENT: Well, I've taken two of your courses and so I know I would enjoy sitting in on your freshman composition and literature lectures. I know that by taking notes for the course, I will improve my own organization. I also think that your method of evaluating students' exams and essays is very fair. Besides, I'd like to be an English teacher after I get a master's degree and I think I can learn a lot about teaching from you. Also, I'm doing my senior project on William Faulkner and I thought I might be able to ask you an occasional question.

DR. TAYLOR: I'm sure that if we work together, we will have some time to talk about Faulkner. As you know, there are several applicants for this job, so after I have talked to each of you, I will post the name of my new assistant on my office door. Thank you for coming in.

36 Why does the student want to talk to Dr. Taylor?
37 In what year of studies is the student?
38 What is one of the responsibilities of Dr. Taylor's student assistant?
39 What does the student think of Dr. Taylor as a teacher?
40 What will the student probably do after graduating from college?
41 What is Dr. Taylor going to do?

Questions 42 through 46 are based on the following talk about the Boy Scout organization:

All Americans have heard of the Boy Scouts, but not everyone knows the origin of this well-known organization. In fact, the idea for Boy Scout troops came from a British baron and war hero, Lord Robert Baden-Powell.

During Baden-Powell's military service in India, he began to develop scouting as a branch of army training. In 1899, he published a book called *Aids to Scouting* based on his experience in training military personnel. He soon found that his book was being used to train boys, and so in 1907 he set up an experimental camp for boys where they devoted their time to initiative tests, and to practicing skills such as cooking outdoors, knot-tying, rope-bridge building, swimming, and so forth. The experiment was a success and Baden-Powell published an outline of the way the camp had been run and, in 1908, he wrote another book called *Scouting for Boys*. As a result, Boy Scout troops sprang up all over England and then all over the world.

Baden-Powell left the army in 1910 in order to devote himself fulltime to the Boy Scouts. He was named Chief Scout at the first international Scout jamboree in 1920 and continued to review and advise Scout troops all over the world until 1937 when he retired at the age of eighty.

42 Where were the ideas for the Boy Scouts developed?

43 According to the passage, what was Baden-Powell's reason for leaving the army?
44 What was Baden-Powell's first book, *Aids to Scouting*, about?
45 When did Baden-Powell finally retire?
46 According to the passage, which of the following was NOT one of Baden-Powell's professions?

Questions 47 through 50 are based on the following conversation:

MRS. TURNER: Mr. Philips, I burned my arm when I was ironing. What would you recommend?

MR. PHILIPS: Try this ointment and also take a Vitamin C tablet every day.

MRS. TURNER: Vitamin C? For a burn?

MR. PHILIPS: Yes, a cut or burn, or even a broken leg, will not heal properly without enough Vitamin C. And, anyway, Mrs. Turner, you should be taking a Vitamin C supplement because you're a heavy smoker.

MRS. TURNER: Really? Why do smokers need Vitamin C?

MR. PHILIPS: Cigarette smoking, even tension, for that matter, can cause the plasma levels of Vitamin C in your blood to go down. And since the human body doesn't produce Vitamin C, we have to get it from our food or from a vitamin supplement. Of course, there are plenty of reasons for you to stop smoking, but even non-smokers need an adequate amount of Vitamin C.

47 Where does this conversation take place?
48 What will Mrs. Turner probably buy?
49 Under what circumstances did Mrs. Turner hurt her arm?
50 Based on what Mr. Philips said, who has the greatest need for a Vitamin C supplement?

THIS IS THE END OF THE LISTENING COMPREHENSION PORTION OF THE TEST. LOOK AT THE TIME NOW, BEFORE YOU BEGIN WORK ON SECTION 2. USE *EXACTLY 25 MINUTES* TO WORK ON SECTION 2.

Practice Test II

Print your name in the box provided at the top of the answer sheet. Print your family name, (or surname), first. Then print your first name. You will now have fifteen seconds to do this:

[15 second pause]

Now open your book at Practice Test II and listen to the directions for the Listening Comprehension Section:

Practice Test II: Section 1
Listening Comprehension

In this section of the test, you will have an opportunity to demonstrate your ability to understand spoken English. There are three parts to this section, with special directions for each part.

Part A

Directions: For each problem in Part A, you will hear a short statement. The statements will be spoken just one time. They will not be written out for you, and you must listen carefully in order to understand what the speaker says.

When you hear a statement, read the four sentences in your test book and decide which one is closest in meaning to the statement you have heard. Then, on your answer sheet, find the number of the problem and mark your answer.

Listen to the following example:

You will hear:
I certainly think the suggestion is worthy of consideration.

You will read: (A) Consideration was given to all suggestions.
(B) Your idea is worth a considerable amount of money.
(C) That sounds like a pretty good idea.
(D) I'm not certain that I like your idea.

Sentence (C), "That sounds like a pretty good idea," means most nearly the same as the statement "I certainly think the suggestion is worthy of consideration." Therefore, you should choose answer (C).

Listen to the next example:

You will hear:
Pamela is quite a bit taller than her sister Ellen was at her age.

You will read: (A) Ellen quit growing at Pamela's age.
(B) Pamela is short for her age.
(C) Pamela and Ellen are the same height.
(D) Ellen is older than Pamela.

Sentence (D) "Ellen is older than Pamela," is closest in meaning to the sentence "Pamela is quite a bit taller than her sister Ellen was at her age." Therefore, you should choose answer (D).

Now let us begin Part A with question number one:

1 He threw up his hands in horror when he saw the aftermath of the hurricane.

2 During the last school year, Ray not only changed his major three times but also went out for football.

3 Even if I had her address, there's no way I could get to her apartment by eight.

4 Rob caught sight of Diane just as he was leaving the building.

5 What have you been up to since I saw you last month?

6 Cathy hasn't read the assignment and neither have I.

7 John gained about ten pounds over the holidays so he's going on a diet.

8 Jim gave up smoking for the New Year.

9 After we have the house painted, we're going to have a big party.

10 Jeff plans to take up tennis during our summer break.

11 In the event of an emergency, break the glass and call the principal.

12 The pilot was forced to circle the airport for two hours because of heavy ground fog.

13 Give Mrs. Johnson her shots before every meal to calm her down.

14 The big room was filled with the odor of cheap wine and cigar smoke.

15 Thank you. It's delicious, but I've had two slices already.

16 When Tom completed his training, he was forced to look for work.

17 He'll never make it back in time for the play this evening.

18 It's only seven, but we've already had dinner and put the baby to bed.

19 There are quite a few new students in my classes this semester.

20 Kay isn't nearly the cook her husband is.

This is the end of Part A.
Now listen to the directions for Part B, as they are read to you:

Part B

<u>Directions</u>: In Part B you will hear fifteen short conversations between two speakers. At the end of each conversation, a third voice will ask a question about what was said. The question will be <u>spoken</u> just one time. After you hear a conversation and the question about it, read the four possible answers and decide which one would be the best response to the question you have heard. Then, on your answer sheet, find the number of the problem and mark your answer.

Listen to the following example:

You will hear:

WOMAN: Isn't this a mistake on my check? I didn't have anything costing $1.30. Look.
MAN: No, Madam. That's the service charge.

QUESTION: Where did the conversation take place?

You will read: (A) In a restaurant.
(B) In a bank.
(C) In a supermarket.
(D) In a service station.

From the conversation we know that the woman is asking about her bill in a restaurant. The best answer, then, is (A), "In a restaurant." Therefore, you should choose answer (A).

Now let us begin Part B with question number 21:

21   MAN: This room is so crowded. I can hardly hear and I can't see a thing.

       WOMAN: I don't understand why they didn't have this show in a bigger theater, do you?

       QUESTION: Why is the man complaining?

22   WOMAN: Your hair looks lovely, Karen. Did you style it yourself?

       KAREN: I wish I had, but I can't do it this way. My neighbor gave me the name of a new beauty salon.

       QUESTION: Who fixed Karen's hair?

23   WOMAN: The northeast is experiencing a really terrible winter. Fuel supplies are running low and a lot of people can't even keep their houses adequately heated.

       MAN: I guess that's why fuel prices have gone up across the nation.

       QUESTION: What is the problem?

24   MAN: I can hardly breathe. Would you please put your cigarette out?

       WOMAN: I'm sorry that I'm bothering you, but this *is* the smoking section. Why don't you ask the stewardess to change your seat?

       QUESTION: What does the woman think the man should do?

25   MAN: Are you going to study after supper, Mary, or would you like to come to the Ritz with us?

       MARY: Thanks, but I can't. Anyway, I've already seen the movie they're showing there.

       QUESTION: What is Mary going to do?

26   WOMAN: Diane didn't get the raise she asked for so she's given notice at the office.

       MAN: She's done the right thing. She'll be able to get a much better position if she goes to another firm.

       QUESTION: What can be said about Diane?

27   MAN: May I take a make-up exam next week?

       WOMAN: It's not my policy to give make-up exams, but the circumstances in your case are exceptional.

       QUESTION: What can be concluded from this conversation?

28   WOMAN: I'm really sorry I didn't make it to your dinner party last
                night, Julie.
       JULIE: It's all very well to say that now; we wasted half the
                evening waiting for you to turn up.

   QUESTION: How did Julie respond?

29   MAN: The switch in the bathroom is broken and we need a new
                socket for the porch light.
     WOMAN: Why don't you get Mr. Kidder to come and take a look?

   QUESTION: What does Mr. Kidder do?

30   MAN: Let's go for a nice long walk into the country this
                morning.
     WOMAN: I certainly could use the exercise, but I think I'm catching
                a cold.

   QUESTION: What will the woman probably do?

31   WOMAN: Edward has completed only about half of his research
                paper for art history class.
       MAN: Well, that's more than I can say for myself.

   QUESTION: What conclusion can be drawn from the man's
                statement?

32   WOMAN: I used to be afraid of heights. Every time I was in a tall
                building or on a bridge, my knees would begin to shake.
       MAN: I had the same problem until I took up mountain
                climbing.

   QUESTION: What did the man and woman say about heights?

33   WOMAN: I feel very uneasy about trusting David with our money.
                How about you?
       MAN: Some people say he's not reliable, but others have a lot of
                confidence in him. I'm willing to give him the benefit of
                the doubt.

   QUESTION: What did the man mean?

34   WOMAN: Mr. Carson, Dr. Brown will have to change your
                appointment to tomorrow at the same time. He's still
                waiting for a flight out of New York.
MR. CARSON: Oh, well, thank you for calling. I'll see you in his office
                then.

   QUESTION: Where is Dr. Brown now?

35   MAN: I had to have Mr. Sloan come over and adjust my TV again last night.

      WOMAN: Maybe it's not your set. If I were you, I'd have someone else check it out.

      QUESTION: What does the woman think the man should do?

This is the end of Part B.
Now look at the directions for Part C as they are read to you:

Part C

Directions: In this part of the test, you will hear several short talks and/or conversations. After each talk or conversation, you will be asked some questions. The talks and questions will be spoken just one time. They will not be written out for you, so you will have to listen carefully in order to understand and remember what the speaker says.

When you hear a question, read the four possible answers in your test book and decide which one would be the best answer to the question you have heard. Then, on your answer sheet, find the number of the problem and fill in (blacken) the space that corresponds to the letter of the answer you have chosen.

Listen to this sample talk:

As president of the Spelunkers Club, I would like to welcome our new members and give you some of our club rules which will make your cave and pothole exploration fun and a little less dangerous.

Because our interest in underground streams, stalactites and stalagmites, and cave insects leads us into unknown places, we always explore in groups of four or more people, two of whom should be experienced spelunkers. We begin our adventure after obtaining permission to enter a particular place and after telling someone outside our expected time of return.

Caves are cold and a trip may last as long as eight hours, so explorers must wear plenty of warm clothing and pack a good supply of food.

Caves are also dark, so each member of the party must have a good light attached to a miner's helmet, extra batteries and bulbs, and, as a further precaution, a few candles and matches in a waterproof container.

Now listen to the first question on the sample talk:

You will hear:
What is the speaker's purpose?

You will read: (A) To attract new members to the Spelunker's Club.
                (B) To gain permission to enter caves and potholes.
                (C) To describe a typical trip through a cave.
                (D) To give new members some useful information.

The best answer to the question, "What is the speaker's purpose?" is (D), "To give new members some useful information." Therefore, you should choose answer (D).

Now listen to the second question on the sample talk:
You will hear:
What can best be said about the guidelines referred to here?

You will read: (A) They are only important for the new members.
(B) They are important to the safety of all spelunkers.
(C) They must be followed in order to find cave insects.
(D) If followed, they eliminate any danger involved in spelunking.

The best answer to the question. "What can best be said about the guidelines referred to here?" is (B), "They are important to the safety of all spelunkers." Therefore, you should choose answer (B).

Questions 36 through 41 refer to the following talk about the brown pelican:

The brown pelican was listed as an endangered species in the United States in 1973. Since that time, the numbers of this coastal bird have increased, principally because of restrictions on the use of the pesticides DDT and endrin.

But even without interference from humans, there are many factors which influence the survival of brown pelican babies.

An adult brown pelican must catch about 20 percent of its body weight in fish every day for its own survival, and the first 11 to 12 weeks after their chicks are hatched, the mother and father together must find another 125 pounds of fish if they have three babies. After that period of tender loving care, the parents abandon the fledglings who then must learn to dive for fish for themselves. These young birds have a certain amount of fat stored in their bodies to get them through this experimental stage, but even so, fewer than 35 out of 100 fledglings learn to feed themselves well enough to survive during that first lonely year.

36 What is the main topic of the talk?
37 According to the speaker, what change has occurred in the brown pelican's environment since 1973?
38 How much fish does an adult brown pelican need per day?
39 What can best be said about brown pelicans as parents?
40 What can be said about the fledgling stage?
41 Why is the amount of stored body fat significant for fledglings?

Questions 42 through 46 are based on the following conversation:

CLERK: May I help you with something?
CUSTOMER: Yes, I'm looking for a dress to wear to my son's graduation. I'd like something formal, but not severe.
CLERK: We have some lovely dresses, but for this weather, I'd recommend a linen suit in a light color. May I show you one in your size?
CUSTOMER: Yes, thank you. I wear size 12. Is linen difficult to take care of?

CLERK: This suit is very easy to care for because the fabric is a linen-polyester blend so it doesn't wrinkle so easily as 100 percent linen and requires little or no ironing. You can wash the suit by hand or machine-wash it on the gentle cycle. In either case, use cold water and a mild detergent and do *not* put the suit in an electric clothes dryer. I think you'll find this fabric durable and quite easy to look after.

CUSTOMER: I like the fabric very much. It has a very nice texture and it's certainly the right weight for this season. May I try it on?

CLERK: Of course. The fitting room is right here on the left.

42 Where does this conversation take place?
43 What is the customer looking for?
44 What can best be said to describe the service the clerk gives the customer?
45 What can best be said about the fabric the suit is made of?
46 What does the customer think of the suit?

Questions 47 through 50 are based on the following speech:

Today, it is my privilege to present an award to a student who we believe has used his or her talent to the fullest. We have named our award the Helen Keller Scholarship to honor extraordinary accomplishment in the face of severe handicaps.

Imagine becoming blind, deaf, and mute before you were two years old. That is what happened to Helen Keller as the result of a serious illness when she was nineteen months old.

Fortunately, Helen's parents took her to Alexander Graham Bell when she was about six, and he recommended a teacher, Miss Anne Sullivan, who was partially blind and had been totally blind. With the constant instruction and devoted companionship of Miss Sullivan, Helen was able to use her talents to the fullest.

She learned to read, write, and speak and eventually graduated from Radcliffe College with honors. Her education and training represent an almost miraculous achievement for a person so handicapped.

Helen Keller, of course, also learned that there were many other people like her, and she subsequently devoted her life to their welfare. She wrote many books and articles and lectured about her life. Her work gave comfort and encouragement to other handicapped people who otherwise might have led a silent, hopeless existence.

47 What is the speaker's stated purpose?
48 What can best be said about Anne Sullivan?
49 Why was the scholarship named after Helen Keller?
50 According to the passage, how have other people benefited from Helen Keller's work?

THIS IS THE END OF THE LISTENING COMPREHENSION PORTION OF THE TEST. LOOK AT THE TIME NOW, BEFORE YOU BEGIN WORK ON SECTION 2. USE *EXACTLY 25 MINUTES* TO WORK ON SECTION 2.

Key for Section 1:
Listening Comprehension

Exercise L–1

1	S	6	G
2	M	7	S
3	G	8	M
4	M	9	G
5	S	10	S

Exercise L–2

1	V	6	S
2	M	7	M
3	S	8	V
4	M	9	S
5	V	10	S

Exercise L–3

1	D	6	S
2	S	7	S
3	S	8	S
4	S	9	S
5	D	10	S

Exercise L–4

1	B	6	A
2	B	7	A
3	B	8	A
4	B	9	A
5	A	10	B

Exercise L–5

1	B	6	B
2	A	7	B
3	A	8	A
4	B	9	A
5	A	10	B

Exercise L–6

1	F	9	F
2	T	10	F
3	F	11	T
4	F	12	F
5	F	13	T
6	T	14	T
7	T	15	T
8	T		

Exercise L–7

1	T	9	T
2	F	10	F
3	F	11	F
4	F	12	F
5	T	13	T
6	T	14	F
7	T	15	F
8	F		

Exercise L–8

1	T	9	T
2	T	10	F
3	T	11	F
4	F	12	F
5	F	13	T
6	T	14	T
7	F	15	T
8	T		

Exercise L–9

1	B	8	B	15	A	22 B
2	B	9	A	16	A	23 A
3	B	10	A	17	A	24 A
4	B	11	A	18	A	25 B
5	B	12	A	19	B	
6	A	13	A	20	A	
7	B	14	A	21	B	

Exercise L–10

1	A	8	B	15	A	22 B
2	A	9	B	16	B	23 B
3	A	10	B	17	B	24 A
4	B	11	B	18	A	25 B
5	B	12	A	19	A	
6	A	13	B	20	B	
7	B	14	A	21	A	

Exercise L–11

1 B	6 B	11 B	16 B
2 B	7 A	12 A	17 A
3 A	8 A	13 A	18 A
4 A	9 B	14 A	19 A
5 B	10 B	15 A	20 B

Exercise L–12

1 B	6 B	11 B	16 A
2 B	7 A	12 A	17 A
3 B	8 B	13 B	18 A
4 B	9 A	14 B	19 A
5 B	10 A	15 B	20 A

Exercise L–13

1 T	9 F
2 T	10 T
3 F	11 T
4 F	12 F
5 T	13 T
6 F	14 T
7 F	15 T
8 T	

Exercise L–14

1 F	9 F
2 T	10 T
3 T	11 T
4 F	12 F
5 T	13 F
6 F	14 T
7 F	15 F
8 T	

Exercises L–15 through L–29, Set A

Exercise L–15, Set A

1 A	6 B
2 B	7 A
3 B	8 A
4 B	9 B
5 A	10 B

Exercise L–16, Set A

1 A	6 A
2 B	7 B
3 B	8 A
4 A	9 B
5 A	10 A

Exercise L–17, Set A

1 A	6 B
2 A	7 A
3 A	8 A
4 A	9 A
5 B	10 B

Exercise L–18, Set A

1 A	6 B
2 B	7 A
3 A	8 A
4 B	9 B
5 B	10 A

Exercise L–19, Set A

1 B	6 A
2 B	7 A
3 B	8 A
4 A	9 A
5 A	10 B

Exercise L–20, Set A

1 A	6 A
2 B	7 B
3 B	8 B
4 B	9 B
5 B	10 B

Exercise L–21, Set A

1 A	6 A
2 B	7 A
3 A	8 B
4 A	9 A
5 A	10 B

Exercise L–22, Set A

1 A	6 B
2 A	7 A
3 A	8 A
4 A	9 A
5 B	10 A

Exercise L–23, Set A

1	B	6	B
2	A	7	B
3	A	8	A
4	A	9	B
5	B	10	A

Exercise L–24, Set A

1	B	6	A
2	A	7	A
3	A	8	A
4	A	9	A
5	A	10	A

Exercise L–25, Set A

1	B	6	A
2	B	7	A
3	B	8	B
4	A	9	B
5	B	10	B

Exercise L–26, Set A

1	A	6	A
2	A	7	A
3	A	8	B
4	B	9	A
5	B	10	A

Exercise L–27, Set A

1	B	6	B
2	A	7	A
3	B	8	B
4	B	9	B
5	B	10	B

Exercise L–28, Set A

1	A	6	A
2	A	7	A
3	A	8	A
4	B	9	A
5	A	10	B

Exercise L–29, Set A

1	A	6	B
2	B	7	A
3	A	8	B
4	B	9	A
5	B	10	A

Exercises L–15 through L–29, Set B

Exercise L–15, Set B

1	A	6	B
2	B	7	B
3	B	8	B
4	A	9	A
5	B	10	A

Exercise L–16, Set B

1	B	6	B
2	A	7	A
3	B	8	A
4	B	9	B
5	B	10	A

Exercise L–17, Set B

1	B	6	B
2	A	7	A
3	B	8	A
4	A	9	B
5	A	10	B

Exercise L–18, Set B

1	A	6	B
2	A	7	B
3	A	8	B
4	A	9	A
5	B	10	A

Exercise L–19, Set B

1	B	6	B
2	B	7	B
3	B	8	A
4	A	9	A
5	A	10	A

Exercise L–20, Set B

1	B	6	A
2	B	7	B
3	B	8	A
4	A	9	B
5	A	10	A

Exercise L–21, Set B

1 B	6 A
2 B	7 A
3 B	8 B
4 B	9 A
5 A	10 A

Exercise L–22, Set B

1 A	6 A
2 B	7 A
3 A	8 B
4 B	9 A
5 A	10 B

Exercise L–23, Set B

1 A	6 A
2 B	7 A
3 B	8 A
4 A	9 A
5 B	10 A

Exercise L–24, Set B

1 B	6 B
2 B	7 B
3 A	8 A
4 B	9 B
5 A	10 A

Excrcise L–25, Set B

1 B	6 A
2 A	7 A
3 A	8 A
4 B	9 B
5 A	10 A

Exercise L–26, Set B

1 B	6 A
2 B	7 B
3 B	8 A
4 B	9 A
5 A	10 B

Exercise L–27, Set B

1 B	6 B
2 A	7 A
3 B	8 A
4 B	9 A
5 B	10 B

Exercise L–28, Set B

1 A	6 B
2 B	7 A
3 A	8 A
4 A	9 B
5 A	10 A

Exercise L–29, Set B

1 A	6 A
2 B	7 B
3 A	8 A
4 A	9 A
5 B	10 B

Exercises L–30 through L–45, Set A

Exercise L–30, Set A

1 A	6 B
2 B	7 A
3 B	8 B
4 A	9 A
5 A	10 B

Exercise L–31, Set A

1 A	6 B
2 B	7 B
3 A	8 B
4 A	9 B
5 B	10 B

Exercise L–32, Set A

1 B	6 A
2 B	7 A
3 A	8 A
4 A	9 B
5 A	10 B

Exercise L–33, Set A

1 B	6 B
2 A	7 B
3 A	8 B
4 B	9 A
5 A	10 B

Exercise L–34, Set A

1 A	6 A
2 B	7 B
3 B	8 B
4 A	9 B
5 B	10 A

Exercise L–35, Set A

1 A	6 B
2 B	7 A
3 A	8 A
4 A	9 A
5 B	10 B

Exercise L–36, Set A

1 A	6 A
2 A	7 B
3 A	8 B
4 A	9 A
5 A	10 A

Exercise L–37, Set A

1 B	6 B
2 B	7 A
3 A	8 B
4 A	9 A
5 A	10 B

Exercise L–38, Set A

1 A	6 B
2 B	7 A
3 A	8 B
4 B	9 B
5 A	10 B

Exercise L–39, Set A

1 B	6 A
2 A	7 B
3 B	8 A
4 B	9 B
5 B	10 A

Exercise L–40, Set A

1 A	6 A
2 A	7 B
3 B	8 A
4 A	9 B
5 B	10 B

Exercise L–41, Set A

1 A
2 A
3 A
4 A
5 A

Exercise L–42, Set A

1 A
2 B
3 A
4 B
5 B

Exercise L–43, Set A

1 B
2 A
3 A
4 B
5 B

Exercise L–44, Set A

1 B
2 B
3 B
4 B
5 B

Exercise L–45, Set A

1 B
2 B
3 A
4 A
5 B

Exercises L–30 through L–45, Set B

Exercise L–30, Set B

1 B	6 B
2 A	7 B
3 A	8 A
4 A	9 A
5 A	10 B

Exercise L–31, Set B

1 B	6 A
2 B	7 A
3 A	8 A
4 B	9 A
5 A	10 B

Exercise L–32, Set B

1 A	6 A
2 B	7 A
3 B	8 B
4 A	9 B
5 A	10 A

Exercise L–33, Set B

1 B	6 A
2 B	7 B
3 A	8 B
4 B	9 B
5 A	10 A

Exercise L–34, Set B

1 B	6 A
2 B	7 A
3 B	8 A
4 B	9 A
5 B	10 A

Exercise L–35, Set B

1 B	6 A
2 A	7 B
3 B	8 B
4 A	9 A
5 A	10 B

Exercise L–36, Set B

1 A	6 B
2 B	7 B
3 A	8 A
4 A	9 B
5 A	10 B

Exercise L–37, Set B

1 A	6 B
2 A	7 A
3 B	8 A
4 A	9 A
5 A	10 B

Exercise L–38, Set B

1 A	6 B
2 A	7 B
3 B	8 A
4 A	9 A
5 B	10 B

Exercise L–39, Set B

1 B	6 B
2 A	7 A
3 B	8 B
4 A	9 A
5 B	10 A

Exercise L–40, Set B

1 B	6 A
2 B	7 A
3 A	8 B
4 A	9 B
5 B	10 A

Exercise L–41, Set B

1 B
2 A
3 B
4 B
5 B

Exercise L–42, Set B

1 A
2 B
3 A
4 A
5 B

Exercise L–43, Set B

1 B
2 A
3 B
4 A
5 B

Exercise L–44, Set B

1 B
2 B
3 B
4 A
5 A

Exercise L–45, Set B

1 B
2 A
3 B
4 B
5 A

Exercises L–46 through L–50, Set A

Exercise L–46, Set A
1 B	6 B
2 A	7 A
3 C	8 C
4 D	9 D
5 C	10 B

Exercise L–47, Set A
1 A	6 C
2 C	7 A
3 B	8 B
4 A	9 A
5 B	10 C

Exercise L–48, Set A
1 D	6 D
2 B	7 A
3 B	8 C
4 C	9 B
5 A	10 B

Exercise L–49, Set A
1 B	6 B
2 A	7 C
3 D	8 A
4 C	9 B
5 B	10 C

Exercise L–50, Set A
1 B	6 C
2 A	7 D
3 A	8 A
4 C	9 B
5 D	10 A

Exercises L–46 through L–50, Set B

Exercise L–46, Set B
1 C	6 A
2 D	7 D
3 C	8 A
4 D	9 D
5 D	10 B

Exercise L–47, Set B
1 C	6 A
2 B	7 B
3 A	8 C
4 C	9 B
5 A	10 B

Exercise L–48, Set B
1 A	6 B
2 B	7 C
3 D	8 A
4 D	9 A
5 B	10 B

Exercise L–49, Set B
1 C	6 A
2 B	7 B
3 D	8 A
4 D	9 A
5 A	10 A

Exercise L–50, Set B
1 C	6 C
2 D	7 B
3 A	8 D
4 C	9 D
5 B	10 C

Exercise L–51
1 B	6 C
2 C	7 B
3 C	8 B
4 C	9 A
5 A	10 C

Exercise L–52
1 A	6 C
2 A	7 C
3 B	8 B
4 D	9 A
5 A	10 C

Exercise L–53
1 D	6 C
2 C	7 B
3 A	8 C
4 B	9 D
5 D	10 B

Exercise L–54

1 D	6 B
2 C	7 C
3 A	8 B
4 C	9 D
5 B	10 A

Exercise L–55

1 C	6 B
2 C	7 B
3 B	8 A
4 A	9 D
5 D	10 C

Exercise L–56

1 A	6 B
2 B	7 A
3 D	8 D
4 B	9 A
5 C	10 B

Exercise L–57

1 C	6 B
2 D	7 B
3 D	8 A
4 C	9 C
5 A	10 C

Exercise L–58

different: are, have, key
1 face, page, fade, age
2 wait, brain, mail, raise
3 lay, pay, delay, say
4 neighbor, eight, weigh, freight
5 prey, hey, they, grey

Exercise L–59

different: steak, great, friend
1 these, gene, theme, scene
2 heel, flee, fee, breeze
3 breathe, lease, grease, flea
4 yield, niece, chief, lien
5 seize, either, ceiling, protein

Exercise L–60

different: give, machine, sunny
1 spine, file, recline, hive
2 sigh, delight, thigh, slight
3 my, rely, comply, spy
4 lie, pie, died, vie
5 dye, bye, eye, rye

Exercise L–61

different: how, now, cost
1 note, spoke, cone, globe
2 most, yolk, roll, don't
3 coat, oats, loan, float
4 foe, toe, doe, hoe
5 know, flow, bowl, owe

Exercise L–62

different: built, pull, but
1 cute, huge, ruler, crude
2 true, clue, due, hue
3 few, crew, stew, spew
4 suit, juice, cruise, fruit
5 feud, neutral, eulogy, neuter

Exercise L–63

1 A	6 A
2 B	7 A
3 B	8 B
4 A	9 B
5 A	10 B

Exercise L–64

1 B	6 B
2 A	7 A
3 A	8 A
4 A	9 B
5 B	10 B

Exercise L–65

1 B	6 A
2 B	7 B
3 A	8 A
4 A	9 B
5 B	10 B

Exercise L–66

1 B	6 B
2 A	7 A
3 B	8 B
4 B	9 A
5 B	10 A

Exercise L–67

1 B	6 B
2 B	7 B
3 A	8 A
4 A	9 A
5 B	10 B

Exercise L–68

1 B	6 A
2 B	7 B
3 A	8 A
4 B	9 B
5 A	10 A

Exercise L–69

1 A	6 B
2 B	7 A
3 A	8 B
4 B	9 B
5 B	10 A

Exercise L–70

1 B	6 A
2 A	7 B
3 A	8 B
4 A	9 A
5 A	10 B

Exercise L–71

1 B	6 A
2 A	7 A
3 A	8 A
4 B	9 B
5 B	10 A

Exercise L–72

1 B	6 B
2 B	7 B
3 A	8 B
4 A	9 A
5 A	10 A

Exercise L–73

1 C, G	6 A, H
2 D, H	7 B, G
3 B, G	8 C, H
4 B, F	9 B, E
5 A, C	10 E, H

Exercise L–74

1 P	6 D	11 U	16 U
2 D	7 D	12 L	17 L
3 D	8 P	13 U	18 L
4 P	9 P	14 U	19 U
5 P	10 D	15 L	20 L

Exercise L–75

1 A	6 S	11 P	16 M
2 S	7 A	12 M	17 P
3 S	8 A	13 P	18 M
4 A	9 S	14 M	19 P
5 A	10 S	15 P	20 M

Exercise L–76

1 C	6 C	11 T	16 T
2 C	7 C	12 S	17 T
3 R	8 R	13 S	18 S
4 C	9 R	14 T	19 T
5 R	10 R	15 S	20 S

Exercise L–77

1 B	6 C	11 C	16 C
2 A	7 B	12 D	17 D
3 C	8 D	13 A	18 A
4 D	9 B	14 B	19 D
5 A	10 A	15 D	20 B

Exercise L–78

1 C	6 D	11 B	16 C
2 A	7 B	12 C	17 D
3 D	8 C	13 D	18 B
4 C	9 A	14 A	19 A
5 A	10 D	15 B	20 A

Exercises L–79 through L–83, Set A

Exercise L–79, Set A

1 B	6 A
2 D	7 D
3 D	8 C
4 A	9 C
5 B	10 B

Exercise L–80, Set A

1 B	6 D
2 C	7 C
3 A	8 D
4 B	9 C
5 D	10 A

Exercise L–81, Set A

1 D	6 C
2 B	7 D
3 B	8 A
4 A	9 D
5 A	10 C

Exercise L–82, Set A

1 C	6 C
2 D	7 C
3 A	8 C
4 A	9 B
5 A	10 A

Exercise L–83, Set A

1 A	6 C
2 C	7 B
3 A	8 C
4 D	9 C
5 C	10 A

Exercises L–79 through L–83, Set B

Exercise L–79, Set B

1 B	6 B
2 B	7 C
3 D	8 A
4 C	9 D
5 D	10 A

Exercise L–80, Set B

1 A	6 A
2 A	7 A
3 D	8 B
4 B	9 C
5 B	10 A

Exercise L–81, Set B

1 B	6 D
2 B	7 D
3 A	8 D
4 C	9 A
5 D	10 C

Exercise L–82, Set B

1 B	6 D
2 C	7 D
3 A	8 C
4 B	9 C
5 A	10 B

Exercise L–83, Set B

1 C	6 B
2 B	7 A
3 A	8 A
4 D	9 C
5 D	10 B

Exercises L–84 through L–87

Exercise L–84

1 C	6 A
2 D	7 C
3 A	8 C
4 B	9 B
5 D	10 A

Exercise L–85

1 R	6 O
2 R	7 O
3 O	8 R
4 R	9 O
5 O	10 R

Exercise L–86

1 A	6 C
2 D	7 A
3 C	8 B
4 D	9 D
5 B	10 C

Exercise L–87

1 C
2 D
3 A
4 D
5 B

Exercises L–88 through L–90, Set A

Exercise L–88, Set A

1 B	6 A
2 B	7 A
3 A	8 A
4 A	9 A
5 B	10 A

Exercise L–89, Set A

1 B	6 B
2 B	7 B
3 A	8 A
4 B	9 B
5 A	10 B

Exercise L–90, Set A

1 A	6 A
2 A	7 A
3 B	8 A
4 A	9 B
5 B	10 B

Exercises L–88 through L–90, Set B

Exercise L–88, Set B

1	D	6	D
2	B	7	C
3	C	8	D
4	B	9	B
5	A	10	A

Exercise L–89, Set B

1	B	6	C
2	D	7	B
3	D	8	B
4	C	9	C
5	A	10	A

Exercise L–90, Set B

1	D	6	A
2	C	7	D
3	A	8	C
4	B	9	D
5	B	10	A

Exercises L–91 through L–95

Exercise L–91

1	A, C	6	B, C
2	D, D	7	A, B
3	B, C	8	A, B
4	C, B	9	D, A
5	C, A	10	B, D

Exercise L–92

1	C, D	6	B, A
2	D, D	7	B, C
3	D, C	8	C, D
4	C, B	9	A, D
5	A, B	10	D, C

Exercise L–93

1	D, B	6	A, C
2	A, D	7	B, C
3	B, A	8	C, B
4	B, A	9	D, D
5	C, B	10	C, A

Exercise L–94

1	B	6	A
2	A	7	A
3	C	8	A
4	A	9	A
5	A	10	B

Exercise L–95

1	A	6	B
2	C	7	B
3	B	8	A
4	C	9	B
5	C	10	C

Exercises L–96 through L–100

Note: There may be additional clues about the location of the person speaking beyond those listed in this key. They should be discussed in class with the group as a whole after exercises L–96 through L–100 have been completed.

Exercise L–96

1 A: airport security guard
2 B: inside front cover
3 A: ticket
4 P: twenty-cent stamps
5 B: biography
6 P: send, flyers, 4th class
7 A: flight
8 P: send, air mail, special delivery
9 A: arrival, departure
10 B: anything on . . . for children

Exercise L–97

1 B: bathing suit
2 R: shrimp cocktails, table
3 H: visiting hours
4 H: maternity ward
5 B: get out, cramp
6 H: nurse
7 R: seafood
8 B: sand castle
9 R: waitress
10 H: shots

Exercise L-98

1 B: hairspray, wash and set
2 H: nails
3 L: fabric softener
4 B: sit under the dryer
5 L: washer, dryer
6 B: bleaching, hair
7 H: paint
8 H: varnish, re-paint, table
9 B: nails, polish
10 L: clean, machine

Exercise L-99

1 T: opening night
2 S: tuition, register
3 B: deposits
4 T: critics, show
5 S: teacher
6 B: deposit
7 S: class
8 T: curtain went up
9 S: call the roll
10 B: interest

Exercise L-100

1 H: bags
2 G: center, superstar
3 S: aisle
4 S: extra bag, ice cream
5 H: staying with us
6 S: one pound of chipped ham, strip steaks
7 G: basketball team
8 H: check-out time
9 G: body-building equipment
10 S: express check-out line

Exercise L-101

1 B
2 A
3 D
4 C
5 A
6 B
7 D
8 B
9 C
10 A

Exercise L-102

1 F, A
2 A, B
3 C, C
4 G, E
5 E, G

Exercise L-103

1 B, C, E
2 A, B, C, E
3 B, C, E
4 B, C, E
5 A, B, C, E
6 B, C, E
7 B, C
8 A, B, C, D, E
9 B, C
10 A, B, C, D, E

Exercise L-104

1 B
2 D
3 A
4 C
5 B
6 A
7 B
8 B
9 D
10 C

Exercise L-105

1 A, B, D
2 B, C, E
3 A, D, E
4 A, B, C

Exercise L-106

1 A, B, D   5 C, D, E
2 B, C, D   6 A, C, D
3 B, C, E   7 A, C, E
4 A, D, E   8 A, B, E

Exercise L-107

1.1 C   3.1 A
1.2 A   3.2 C
2.1 B   4.1 B
2.2 B   4.2 A

Exercise L-108

1 √   7 √
2 ×   8 √
3 ×   9 ×
4 √   10 √
5 √   11 ×
6 ×   12 ×

Key for Section 2:
Structure and Written Expression

Exercise S–1
a–1	f–9
b–8	g–4
c–10	h–7
d–2	i–3
e–6	j–5

Exercise S–2
1 B	6 A
2 D	7 A
3 A	8 B
4 C	9 C
5 B	10 D

Exercise S–3
a–2	f-10
b–1	g–6
c–4	h–3
d–5	i–7
e–9	j–8

Exercise S–4
1 N	9 INF
2 PRO	10 PRO
3 INF	11 N
4 G	12 PRO
5 NC	13 NC
6 N	14 G
7 G	15 INF
8 NC	

Exercise S–5
1 is located
2 will interest
3 are
4 stand
5 depart
6 are
7 has . . . installed
8 has been checked out (and) read
9 shone
10 will have been completed
11 lies
12 is
13 held on, walked
14 damaged, caused
15 were
16 instituted
17 should have been
18 lie
19 are . . . blooming
20 have . . . studied

Exercise S–6
1 √√	6 √√	11 √√	16 ×
2 ×	7 √	12 ×	17 √
3 √	8 √	13 √	18 √√
4 √√	9 √√	14 ×	19 √√
5 ×	10 ×	15 √	20 √√

Exercise S–7
1 √	6 ×
2 √	7 ×
3 √	8 ×
4 ×	9 √
5 ×	10 ×

Exercise S–8
1 N	6 N	11 V	16 V
2 N	7 N	12 N	17 V
3 N	8 V	13 V	18 V
4 N	9 N	14 V	19 V
5 V	10 N	15 N	20 V

Exercise S–9
1 C	6 C	11 C	16 C
2 P	7 P	12 P	17 P
3 C	8 C	13 P	18 C
4 P	9 C	14 P	19 P
5 P	10 P	15 C	20 C

Exercise S–10
1 √	6 −	11 −	16 −
2 +	7 √	12 +	17 +
3 −	8 √	13 √	18 √
4 √	9 −	14 −	19 +
5 +	10 +	15 √	20 √

Exercise S–11

1 a common disease
2 in my class
3 a German car
4 such as peaches and watermelon
5 a famous prime minister
6 in this jar
7 of this book
8 the famous soccer player
9 from Cuba
10 the ones in the hall
11 in the hot sun
12 a stimulant
13 a popular pain-killer
14 at me
15 in his condition
16 a famous movie star
17 with red hair
18 such as tomatoes and lettuce
19 according to a recent survey
20 across the street

Exercise S–12

1 A	6 B
2 D	7 D
3 B	8 A
4 C	9 C
5 B	10 C

Exercise S–13

a–6	f–1
b–9	g–4
c–2	h–5
d–8	i–7
e–10	j–3

Exercise S–14

1 a (are viewing)—is viewing
  b (was barking)—were barking
  c (have left)—has left
2 d (was)—has been
  e (has been being)—has been
  f (will work)—would work
3 g (has began)—has begun
  h (has broke)—has broken
  i (sunk)—sank

Exercise S–15

1 is	11 is
2 is	12 are
3 are	13 is
4 is	14 is
5 are	15 are
6 is	16 is
7 is	17 are
8 is	18 is
9 are	19 are
10 is	20 are

Exercise S–16

1 was	6 ×
2 was	7 ×
3 was	8 √
4 was	9 √
5 was	10 ×

Exercise S–17

1 has	6 ×
2 have	7 ×
3 has	8 √
4 has	9 √
5 has	10 ×

Exercise S–18

1 are	6 √
2 is	7 √
3 are	8 ×
4 are	9 ×
5 are	10 ×

Exercise S–19

1 are	6 is
2 is	7 are
3 are	8 is
4 is	9 are
5 is	10 is

Exercise S–20

1 ✕	6 ✕
2 √	7 √
3 ✕	8 √
4 √	9 √
5 ✕	10 ✕

Exercise S–21

1 are	6 are
2 are	7 are
3 is	8 is
4 is	9 are
5 are	10 are

Exercise S–22

1 are	5 are
2 are	6 are
3 is	7 are
4 are	8 are

Exercise S–23

1 stands	11 drink
2 has	12 nests
3 are	13 stand
4 was	14 was
5 is	15 is
6 was	16 remains
7 contributes	17 provides
8 confirms	18 is
9 bear	19 is
10 has	20 are

Exercise S–24

1 B	6 C
2 C	7 C
3 A	8 A
4 C	9 A
5 B	10 D

Exercise S–25

1 ✕	is established	—so far
2 ✕	were closed	—since the end of last summer
3 √	needs	—from time to time
4 ✕	is . . . considering	—for some time now
5 ✕	will leave . . . (and) return	—by this time next year
6 ✕	is found	—up until now
7 √	has been raining	—since yesterday
8 ✕	has . . . been	—at the time of his death
9 √	had finished	—by the end of the hour
10 ✕	are coming	—in the early part of this century

Exercise S–26

1 rung	11 fed
2 √	12 lead
3 chosen	13 swung
4 swore	14 √
5 √	15 fallen
6 become	16 hide
7 √	17 √
8 bitten	18 come
9 shook	19 heard
10 √	20 √

Exercise S–27

1 B	6 A
2 D	7 A
3 B	8 B
4 C	9 C
5 C	10 A

Exercise S–28

a–8	f–1
b–5	g–9
c–2	h–6
d–7	i–10
e–4	j–3

Exercise S–29

1 who/that	6 if
2 which	7 that
3 whom	8 what
4 so that	9 where
5 because	

Exercise S–30

1 MC	11 MC
2 SC	12 SC
3 SC	13 MC
4 SC	14 MC
5 MC	15 MC
6 SC	16 SC
7 MC	17 SC
8 SC	18 SC
9 MC	19 MC
10 SC	20 SC

Exercise S–31

1 PHR	11 PHR
2 SC	12 SC
3 SC	13 PHR
4 PHR	14 SC
5 SC	15 SC
6 SC	16 PHR
7 PHR	17 SC
8 SC	18 SC
9 PHR	19 PHR
10 SC	20 SC

Exercise S–32

1 MC	11 SC
2 SC	12 MC
3 PHR	13 MC
4 PHR	14 PHR
5 MC	15 PHR
6 PHR	16 MC
7 PHR	17 PHR
8 SC	18 SC
9 SC	19 SC
10 PHR	20 MC

Exercise S–33

1 SC	11 PHR
2 PHR	12 PHR
3 SC	13 PHR
4 MC	14 SC
5 SC	15 MC
6 MC	16 PHR
7 SC	17 SC
8 PHR	18 PHR
9 SC	19 SC
10 MC	20 PHR

Exercise S–34

1 ADJ	11 MC
2 MC	12 BOTH
3 BOTH	13 ADJ
4 MC	14 MC
5 MC	15 ADJ
6 ADJ	16 ADJ
7 MC	17 MC
8 MC	18 ADJ
9 ADJ	19 MC
10 ADJ	20 ADJ

Exercise S–35

1 **2 who** . . . utensils; **that** . . . developed
2 **2 that** he . . . elements; **to which** . . . bonded
3 **1 which** . . . alloys
4 **1 that** were . . . processes
5 **2 which** . . . aluminum; **that** . . . marble
6 **2 which** . . . advance; **which** . . . industry
7 **1 which** . . . priceless

8 **2 which** ... metal; **which** ... silver

9 **2 which** ... gold; **when** ... production

10 **1 where** ... developed

Exercise S–36

1 — the United States launched in the 1960's and 1970's—
— NASA could use only once—

2 — engineers designed—

3 — the astronauts rode in—

4 — President Nixon approved in 1972—
— NASA could reuse many times—

5 — NASA selected for the STS program—

6 — the astronauts can control—

7 — NASA had originally scheduled for April 10—

8 — the spacecraft used—

9 — NASA officials chose for the first STS flight—
— he had made—

10 — NASA launched in April 1981—
— the United States will send up in coming years—

Exercise S–37

1 D	6 C	
2 C	7 A	
3 B	8 A	
4 D	9 B	
5 A	10 B	

Exercise S–38

1 **1 Until** ... **invented** (TIME)

2 **1 provided that** ... deadline (CONDITION)

3 **1 whether or not** ... resignation (CONDITION)

4 **1 As** ... cools (TIME)

5 **2 Because** ... years (CAUSE); **since** ... 1946 (TIME)

6 **1 While** ... people (OPPOSITION)

7 **1 although** ... increased (OPPOSITION)

8 **1 Unless** ... Monday (CONDITION)

9 **1 as if** ... time (MANNER)

10 **2 so that** ... repainted (RESULT); **before** ... begins (TIME)

11 **2 In the event that** ... rains (CONDITION); **until** ... again (TIME)

12 **1 even though** ... country (OPPOSITION)

13 **1 Only if** ... afternoon (CONDITION)

14 **2 as soon as** ... know (TIME); **if** ... city (CONDITION)

15 **2 If** ... sleep (CONDITION); **even though** ... sufficient (OPPOSITION)

Exercise S–39

1 D	6 B	
2 A	7 B	
3 A	8 A	
4 D	9 D	
5 A	10 C	

Exercise S—40

1 O that . . . quickly	11 S that . . . dish
2 S that . . . year	12 O that . . . old
3 O that . . . peace	13 O that . . . unfair
4 O that . . . well	14 S that . . . down
5 S that . . . quiz	15 O that . . . virus
6 O that . . . angry	16 O that . . . speeding
7 O that . . . important	17 O that . . . differ
8 S that . . . flat	18 S that . . . exists
9 O that . . . else	19 O that . . . batteries
10 O that . . . perspiration	20 O that . . . soon

Exercise S—41

1 ×	12 NC that his men . . . suspect
2 NC that hard work . . . rewarded	13 NC that the appliance . . . water
3 NC that his plane . . . condition	14 ×
4 NC that people . . . sequence	15 NC that the report . . . accurate
5 ×	16 ×
6 NC that she . . . willingly	17 ×
7 NC that the building . . . equipment	18 NC that the planning commission . . . developers
8 ×	
9 NC that fifteen percent . . . wasted	19 NC that its electric cars . . . trouble-free
10 NC that they . . . hikers	
11 ×	20 NC that the old couch . . . recovering

Exercise S—42

1 S where . . . went	11 O why . . . book
2 O how . . . spent	12 S how . . . vacation
3 S what . . . said	13 O where . . . card
4 O how . . . test	14 S how . . . communicate
5 S what . . . asked	15 O where .. lived
6 O what . . . eat	16 O how . . . formed
7 S where . . . vacation	17 O where . . . times
8 O how . . . costs	18 S how . . . things
9 O why . . . home	19 O how . . . operates
10 O how . . . learn	20 O where . . . located

Exercise S-43

1 NC	11 NC
2 INF	12 INF
3 NC	13 NC
4 NC	14 INF
5 INF	15 NC
6 NC	16 NC
7 INF	17 NC
8 NC	18 INF
9 NC	19 INF
10 INF	20 NC

Exercise S—44

1. 1 that . . . 3100 B.C.
2. 1 that . . . 1836
3. 1 Christians' . . . dead
4. 1 the fact . . . unreliable
5. 1 that . . . purposes
6. 1 why . . . sleeps
7. 1 that . . . heat
8. 1 what . . . earth
9. 1 where . . . begins
10. 1 that . . . safely
11. 1 how . . . feeling
12. 2 what . . . is; how . . . energy
13. 1 where . . . falling
14. 1 that gravity . . . time
15. 2 that . . . discovered; how . . . byproducts
16. 1 what . . . animals
17. 1 there is . . . years
18. 1 that . . . sun
19. 1 that . . . New World
20. 1 how . . . product

Exercise S—45

1 B	5 A
2 A	6 A
3 B	7 B
4 A	8 A

Exercise S—46

1 B	6 A
2 A	7 B
3 B	8 A
4 A	9 B
5 B	10 A

Exercise S—47

1 A	that	NC	6 A	which	ADJ
B	which	ADJ	B	that	NC
2 A	that	NC	7 A	that	NC
B	which	ADJ	B	which	ADJ
3 A	which	ADJ	8 A	which	ADJ
B	that	NC	B	that	NC
4 A	that	NC	9 A	that	NC
B	which	ADJ	B	which	ADJ
5 A	that	NC	10 A	that	NC
B	which	ADJ	B	which	ADJ

Exercise S—48

1 NC	9 NC
2 NC	10 ADJ
3 ADJ	11 NC
4 ADJ	12 NC
5 NC	13 NC
6 ADJ	14 NC
7 NC	15 NC
8 ADJ	

Exercise S-49

1 B	6 B
2 C	7 C
3 A	8 A
4 D	9 C
5 A	10 C

Exercise S—50

1 ADJ	11 NC
2 ADV	12 ADJ
3 NC	13 ADV
4 ADJ	14 ADV
5 NC	15 ADJ
6 ADV	16 NC
7 ADV	17 ADJ
8 ADJ	18 NC
9 ADJ	19 ADV
10 NC	20 ADV

Exercise S—51

1 C	6 D
2 D	7 A
3 A	8 C
4 A	9 A
5 D	10 B

Exercise S-52

1 S	9 CX
2 CX	10 CX
3 CX	11 S
4 S	12 CX
5 CX	13 CX
6 CX	14 S
7 CX	15 S
8 CX	

Exercise S–53

1 S-2	9 S–2
2 S–1	10 CX–4
3 CX–3	11 CX–3
4 CX–4	12 S–2
5 CX–3	13 CX–3
6 S–1	14 CX–4
7 CX–2	15 S–2
8 CX–3	

Exercise S–54

1 A	6 B
2 B	7 A
3 C	8 B
4 B	9 A
5 D	10 A

Exercise S–55

1 which	9 which
2 although	10 which
3 what	11 what
4 although	12 although
5 what	13 what
6 which	14 which
7 what	15 although
8 although	

Exercise S–56

1 √	9 ×
2 ×	10 √
3 √	11 ×
4 ×	12 √
5 ×	13 ×
6 √	14 √
7 √	15 √
8 ×	

Exercise S–57

1 B	6 A
2 A	7 B
3 D	8 A
4 B	9 C
5 A	10 B

Exercise S–58

a–3	f–1
b–10	g–9
c–6	h–2
d–7	i–5
e–4	j–8

Exercise S–59

1 INF	11 INF
2 PREP	12 INF
3 INF	13 INF
4 INF	14 PREP
5 PREP	15 PREP
6 INF	16 PREP
7 INF	17 PREP
8 INF	18 PREP
9 PREP	19 PREP
10 PREP	20 INF

Exercise S–60

1 The <u>cats</u> <u>want</u> (to eat).

2 (To cooperate) with others <u>is</u> important.

3 <u>Settlers</u> <u>came</u> to Texas (to live).

4 <u>They</u> <u>are going</u> (to swim) to shore.

5 <u>Fred</u> <u>wanted</u> (to walk) to school.

6 <u>She</u> <u>tried</u> (to put) her wallet . . .

7 The <u>senators</u> <u>intend</u> (to pass) the bill.

8 <u>She</u> <u>likes</u> (to entertain) often.

9 Students go to school (to learn).   [S: Students, V: go]

10 (To eat) three times a day is healthy.   [S: (To eat), V: is]

11 Smoke tends (to rise) to the ceiling.   [S: Smoke, V: tends]

12 (To drink) while driving is dangerous.   [S: (To drink), V: is]

13 She went to the post office (to mail) some letters.   [S: She, V: went]

14 Scientists hope (to find) a cure for cancer.   [S: Scientists, V: hope]

15 We are going (to have) beautiful weather today.   [S: We, V: are going]

16 She is going (to break) his heart.   [S: She, V: is going]

17 They plan (to move) to the north.   [S: They, V: plan]

18 (To kill) bugs, spray the area carefully. (No S)   [V: spray]

19 They flew to Austin (to see) their friends.   [S: They, V: flew]

20 (To drive) to New York is her plan.   [S: (To drive), V: is]

Exercise S–61

1 (Swimming) is good exercise.   [S: (Swimming), V: is]

2 He has been eating too much.   [S: He, V: has been eating]

3 They go (fishing) every weekend.   [S: They, V: go]

4 Your (writing) is improving little by little.   [S: (writing), V: is improving]

5 He hates (receiving) anonymous notes.   [S: He, V: hates]

6 Teachers despise (cheating).   [S: Teachers, V: despise]

7 (Backpacking) is popular among college students.   [S: (Backpacking), V: is]

8 He can't go out without (drinking) too much.   [S: He, V: can't go]

9 My students are turning in their papers on time this semester.   [S: students, V: are turning]

10 (Rollerskating) on rough pavement invites accidents.   [S: (Rollerskating), V: invites]

11 No one appreciates their (singing) so loudly.   [S: one, V: appreciates]

12 (Gardening) has been becoming more popular.   [S: (Gardening), V: becoming]

13 She thanked me for (helping) her.   [S: She, V: thanked]

14 (Turning) a corner quickly is frightening to pedestrians.   [S: (Turning), V: is frightening]

15 He has obviously been staying up too late.   [S: He, V: been staying]

16 The children are growing tired.   [S: children, V: are growing]

17 (Expecting) too much leads to frustration.   [S: (Expecting), V: leads]

18 (Having) an accident can be costly.   [S: (Having), V: can be]

19 She is developing good (handwriting).   [S: She, V: is developing]

20 (Growing) up can be a difficult experience.   [S: (Growing), V: can be]

Exercise S–62

1 $\overset{\text{s}}{\underline{\text{baby}}}$; $\overset{\text{v}}{\underline{\text{needs}}}$

2 $\overset{\text{s}}{\underline{\text{kangaroo}}}$; $\overset{\text{v}}{\underline{\text{is}}}$

3 $\overset{\text{s1}}{\underline{\text{size}}}$, $\overset{\text{s2}}{\underline{\text{condition}}}$; $\overset{\text{v}}{\underline{\text{make}}}$

4 $\overset{\text{s}}{\underline{\text{kangaroo}}}$; $\overset{\text{v}}{\underline{\text{will encourage}}}$

5 $\overset{\text{s}}{\underline{\text{That}}}$; $\overset{\text{v}}{\underline{\text{will be}}}$

6 $\overset{\text{s}}{\underline{\text{mother}}}$; $\overset{\text{v}}{\underline{\text{will have}}}$

7 $\overset{\text{s1}}{\underline{\text{Living}}}$, $\overset{\text{s2}}{\underline{\text{being fed}}}$; $\overset{\text{v}}{\underline{\text{are}}}$

8 $\overset{\text{v}}{\underline{\text{are}}}$; $\overset{\text{s}}{\underline{\text{animals}}}$

9 $\overset{\text{s}}{\underline{\text{To see}}}$; $\overset{\text{v}}{\underline{\text{is}}}$

10 $\overset{\text{s}}{\underline{\text{baby}}}$; $\overset{\text{v}}{\underline{\text{can be seen}}}$

11 $\overset{\text{s1}}{\underline{\text{warmth}}}$, $\overset{\text{s2}}{\underline{\text{protection}}}$, $\overset{\text{s3}}{\underline{\text{nourishment}}}$; $\overset{\text{v}}{\underline{\text{enable}}}$.

12 $\overset{\text{v}}{\underline{\text{jumps}}}$; $\overset{\text{s}}{\underline{\text{kangaroo}}}$

13 $\overset{\text{s}}{\underline{\text{male}}}$; $\overset{\text{v}}{\underline{\text{will weigh}}}$

14 $\overset{\text{s}}{\underline{\text{To grow}}}$; $\overset{\text{v}}{\underline{\text{is}}}$

15 $\overset{\text{s}}{\underline{\text{skill}}}$; $\overset{\text{v}}{\underline{\text{enables}}}$

16 $\overset{\text{s}}{\underline{\text{kangaroo}}}$; $\overset{\text{v}}{\underline{\text{is}}}$

17 $\overset{\text{s}}{\underline{\text{"Marsupial"}}}$; $\overset{\text{v}}{\underline{\text{means}}}$

18 $\overset{\text{v}}{\underline{\text{are}}}$; $\overset{\text{s}}{\underline{\text{animals}}}$

19 $\overset{\text{s1}}{\underline{\text{Kangaroos}}}$, $\overset{\text{s2}}{\underline{\text{koalas}}}$, $\overset{\text{s3}}{\underline{\text{opposums}}}$; $\overset{\text{v}}{\underline{\text{are}}}$

20 $\overset{\text{s}}{\underline{\text{That these species are protected}}}$; $\overset{\text{v}}{\underline{\text{is}}}$

Exercise S–63

1 (hanging) basket

2 people (suffering); (licensed) psychologist

3 (crying) child; (soothing) words

4 homes (destroyed); (wrecking) crews; (coming) weeks

5 number . . . (provided)

6 (baked) potatoes; (grated) cheese; (fried) bacon

7 movies (shown); movies (produced)

8 (torn) garments; (experienced) seamstress or tailor

9 volunteers (recruited); (lost) hikers; (exhausting) days

10 people (walking); (lighted) areas

Exercise S–64

1 V	11 V
2 V ADJ	12 V ADJ
3 V	13 V ADJ
4 V ADJ	14 V ADJ
5 V	15 V ADJ
6 V	16 V
7 V	17 V
8 V	18 V ADJ
9 V ADJ	19 V
10 V ADJ	20 V ADJ

Exercise S–65

1 frightening horror movies; frightened children
2 the boring speech; the bored audience
3 the amusing clowns; the amused spectators
4 the exhausting ten-mile walk; the exhausted campers
5 the disappointing test grades; the disappointed teacher
6 the surprising gift; the surprised youngster
7 the tiring three-hour class; the tired students
8 the confusing math problem; the confused class
9 the disgusting review; the disgusted artist
10 the lawyer's convincing argument; the convinced jury

Exercise S–66

1 A	6 A
2 A	7 A
3 B	8 B
4 B	9 B
5 B	10 A

Exercise S–67

1 × (filling)	6 × (aspired)
2 √	7 × (assigning)
3 × (boring)	8 √
4 √	9 √
5 √	10 × (boiling)

Exercise S–68

1 While playing outside . . .
2 Having broken his leg . . .
3 After having developed a new drug . . .
4 Having a lot of oil . . .
5 After having arrived at the factory . . .
6 Being easy to mine and refine . . .
7 When threatened . . .
8 Before planting the seeds . . .
9 After having been installed . . .
10 Having a high protein content . . .

Exercise S–69

1 B	6 B
2 A	7 B
3 B	8 A
4 B	9 B
5 A	10 B

Exercise S–70

1 √ winning; Algeria	11 √ placed; plants
2 × awarded; Rene Sully-Prudhomme	12 √ ranging; species
3 × decorated; workers	13 √ grabbed; tail
4 × fleeing; city	14 × running; nose
5 √ located; Cathedral	15 × living; weeks
6 × rejected; windows	16 √ knowing; residents
7 √ forced; shows	17 × riding; accidents
8 × drinking; it	18 √ made; quilts
9 √ formed; alloys	19 × isolated; discovery
10 √ flourishing; musicians	20 × having; destruction

Exercise S–71

1 D	6 A
2 D	7 B
3 B	8 C
4 C	9 A
5 C	10 A

Exercise S–72

a–9	f–5
b–6	g–4
c–7	h–10
d–2	i–3
e–8	j–1

Exercise S–73

1 (him)-he	9 (their)–her
2 (he)–him	10 (their)–its
3 (him)–he	11 (which)/*rewrite*
4 (him)–his	12 (which)/*rewrite*
5 (theirselves)–themselves	13 (which)/*rewrite*
6 (their)–his	14 (which)–who
7 (their)–her	15 (whom)–which
8 (their)–his	

Exercise S–74

1 I	me	my	mine	myself
2 you	you	your	yours	yourself
3 he	him	his	his	himself
4 she	her	her	hers	herself
5 it	it	its	——	itself
6 we	us	our	ours	ourselves
7 you	you	your	yours	yourselves
8 they	them	their	theirs	themselves
9 one	one	one's	——	oneself
10 who	whom	whose	whose	——

Exercise S–75

1 S	6 S
2 PA	7 S
3 O	8 PP
4 O	9 PA
5 R	10 R

Exercise S–76

1 we	6 × (whom)–who
2 they	7 √
3 he	8 √
4 who	9 × (me)–I
5 she	10 × (him)–he

Exercise S–77

1 me	6 × (whom)–who
2 her	7 × (I)–me
3 whom	8 √
4 him	9 √
5 her	10 × (whom)–who

Exercise S–78

1 his	6 × (me)–my
2 her	7 × (whom)–who
3 whose	8 √
4 his	9 √
5 his	10 × (us)–our

Exercise S–79

1 yours	6 × (me)–mine
2 hers	7 √
3 his	8 × (him)–his
4 hers	9 × (me)–mine
5 ours	10 × (your)–yours

Exercise S–80

1 ourselves	6 × (hisself)–himself
2 itself	7 × (ourself)–ourselves
3 oneself	8 √
4 himself	9 √
5 herself	10 × (yourself)–yourselves

Exercise S–81

1 O–4	9 PP–10
2 S–2	10 S-1
3 R–15	11 R–15
4 PA–7	12 PA–8
5 O–5	13 PP–12
6 PP–9	14 R–13
7 S–3	15 PP–11
8 O–6	

Exercise S–82

1 who	11 who
2 her	12 he
3 he	13 mine
4 whom	14 who
5 whom	15 them
6 hers	16 who
7 me	17 himself
8 she	18 me
9 his	19 him
10 him	20 I

Exercise S–83

1 D	6 A
2 B	7 D
3 C	8 A
4 C	9 B
5 A	10 D

Exercise S–84

1 her	6 × (their)–his
2 himself	7 √
3 their	8 × (her)–their
4 he	9 × (my)–our
5 his	10 × (their)–his

Exercise S–85

1 their	6 × (their)–his
2 its	7 \
3 its	8 \
4 its	9 × (their)–his
5 its	10 \

Exercise S–86

1 him	his	11 us	our
2 them	their	12 him	his
3 her	her	13 him	his
4 us	our	14 them	their
5 them	their	15 you	your
6 it	its	16 her	her
7 him	his	17 it	its
8 her	her	18 them	their
9 him	his	19 it	its
10 her	her	20 it	its

Exercise S–87

2 Everyone has to use his identification number to activate the computer.

3 In the bus sit the musicians, each holding his instrument.

4 The boy's blue jeans are so old that they look like a rag.

5 Anyone who abuses his children should be punished for his actions.

6 No one is as ambitious as he who wants to be rich.

7 Both London and Paris are crowded in the summer because they are so famous.

8 The list of special courses is available at the front desk because it is requested by so many students.

9 The hundred thousand dollars was found because the thief dropped it while escaping.

10 The welfare department, as well as other social services, will have its budget cut.

Exercise S–88

1 A	6 B
2 A	7 A
3 B	8 A
4 B	9 B
5 A	10 B

Exercise S–89

1 ×	6 ×	11 √	16 √
2 √	7 √	12 ×	17 √
3 √	8 ×	13 √	18 √
4 ×	9 ×	14 ×	19 ×
5 √	10 √	15 ×	20 √

Exercise S–90

1 ×	6 ×
2 √	7 ×
3 ×	8 ×
4 ×	9 ×
5 √	10 ×

Exercise S–91

1 B	6 A
2 A	7 B
3 A	8 B
4 B	9 B
5 B	10 B

Exercise S-92

1 A	6 B
2 D	7 D
3 B	8 B
4 A	9 C
5 D	10 A

Exercise S–93

1 A	11 A
2 F	12 A
3 √	13 A
4 R	14 R
5 A	15 F
6 R	16 √
7 √	17 √
8 F	18 R
9 A	19 √
10 F	20 F

Exercise S–94

1 B	6 C
2 C	7 C
3 C	8 D
4 C	9 A
5 B	10 B

Exercise S–95

a–8	f–4
b–5	g–7
c–2	h–9
d–1	i–10
e–3	j–6

Exercise S–96

1 (agricultural)–agriculture
2 (separationed)–separated
3 (danger)–dangerous
4 (rapid)–rapidly
5 (extreme)–extremely
6 (erasing)–erasure
7 (sweetly)–sweet
8 (expensivest)–most expensive
9 (inventing)–invention
10 (calmly)–calm

Exercise S–97

1
1 observation
2 information
3 determination
4 formation
5 examination
6 obligation

2
1 concealment
2 movement
3 alignment
4 judgment
5 advertisement
6 encouragement

3
1 dependence
2 inference
3 acceptance
4 existence
5 abhorrence
6 correspondence

4
1 survival
2 removal
3 approval
4 refusal
5 trial
6 withdrawal

5
1 disclosure
2 pressure
3 exposure
4 pleasure
5 erasure
6 failure

6
1 delivery
2 inquiry
3 discovery
4 perjury
5 recovery
6 flattery

Exercise S-98

√ = 1, 3, 5, 6, 7, 10, 13, 19, 21, 24, 25, 27, 28

31 fail
32 remove
33 collect
34 master
35 assist

36 invent
37 depart
38 conclude
39 decorate
40 propose

Exercise S-99

1 earnings
2 preference
3 erasure
4 information
5 surroundings
6 decision
7 refusal
8 recovery
9 agreement
10 joint
11 learning
12 excitement
13 coming
14 division
15 withdrawal
16 implication
17 sitting
18 existence
19 departure
20 leaving

Exercise S-100

1 × resignation
2 √
3 × failure
4 √
5 × discovery
6 √
7 × separation
8 × movement
9 √
10 × development
11 √
12 √
13 × belief
14 × recommendation
15 √
16 × arrangement
17 × repetition
18 × pressure
19 × permission
20 × desegregation

Exercise S-101

abstract	refer to people
employment	employee
service	servant
carpentry	carpenter
racket	racketeer
sociability	socialite
alcoholism	alcoholic
geology	geologist
innovation	innovator
youth	youngster
authorship	authoress

Exercise S-102

nouns	adjectives
ease	easy
fame	famous
truth	truthful
action	active
supplement	supplementary
death	deathly
heroism	heroic
tradition	traditional
statue	statuesque
care	careless
fool	foolish
Texas	Texan
comfort	comfortable
trouble	troublesome
wood	wooden

Exercise S–103

1 yearly	6 metallic
2 silklike	7 penniless
3 eventful	8 musical
4 rocky	9 babyish
5 careless	10 stormy

√ = 11, 13, 14, 15, 17,19, 21, 22, 24, 25, 29, 30

Exercise S-104

adjective	adverb
worldly	beautifully
womanly	carelessly
shapely	nervously
friendly	easily
yearly	seriously
stately	enjoyably
neighborly	finally
ghostly	foolishly
costly	universally
cowardly	passively

Exercise S–105

	verb	noun	adjective	adverb
1	energize	*energy*	energetic	energetically
2	quicken	quickness	*quick*	quickly
3	base	base	basic	*basically*
4	*succeed*	success	successful	successfully
5	electrify	*electricity*	electrical	electrically
6	exclude	exclusion	*exclusive*	exclusively
7	*economize*	economy	economical	economically
8	sense	*sensation*	sensational	sensationally
9	categorize	category	categorical	*categorically*
10	*repeat*	repetition	repetitive	repetitively

Exercise S-106

1 noun–radical
2 adjective–assert
3 noun–preside
4 noun–able
5 verb–winter
6 instructive
7 nationality
8 changeable
9 summarize
10 loneliness

Exercise S–107

1 B		9 B	
2 B		10 B	
3 B		11 A	
4 A		12 B	
5 B		13 B	
6 A		14 A	
7 A		15 A	
8 A			

Exercise S-108

1 sweet	11 quiet
2 silent	12 honest
3 rapidly	13 swiftly
4 angrily	14 slowly
5 easily	15 beautiful
6 pale	16 sad
7 false	17 loose
8 easily	18 nervously
9 crazy	19 lazily
10 good	20 uncontrollably

Exercise S–109

1 careful	6 well
2 carefully	7 cautiously
3 sadly	8 delicious
4 sad	9 finally
5 good	10 final

Exercise S-110

1 ADV–flew
2 ADJ-notes
3 ADV–recommended
4 ADJ–judge
5 ADV–flew
6 ADJ-position
7 ADJ-trees
8 ADV-looked
9 ADJ-look
10 ADJ-jewelry

Exercise S-111

1 real
2 really
3 really
4 really
5 real
6 real
7 really
8 really
9 really
10 real
11 extremely
12 extreme
13 extremely
14 extreme
15 extreme
16 extremely
17 extremely
18 extremely
19 extremely
20 extreme

Exercise S-112

1 A	4 B	7 B	10 B
2 D	5 C	8 D	
3 B	6 C	9 C	

Exercise S–113

1 older, oldest
2 happier, happiest
3 more foolish, most foolish
4 thinner, thinest
5 more enthusiastic, most enthusiastic
6 stranger, strangest
7 crazier, craziest
8 more interesting, most interesting
9 more energetic, most energetic
10 funnier, funniest
11 slower, slowest
12 more regular, most regular
13 messier, messiest
14 more common, most common
15 wiser, wisest
16 more threatened, most threatened
17 cleverer, cleverest
18 noisier, noisiest
19 more distresssing, most distressing
20 more amorous, most amorous

Exercise S–114

× = 1, 3, 4, 8, 10, 11, 14, 16, 17, 20

Exercise S-115

1 √
2 × better
3 × less expensive
4 × quickly
5 × really
6 √
7 √
8 √
9 √
10 √
11 × sweet
12 × skillfully
13 × considerably
14 √
15 × probably
16 √
17 × helpful
18 × extremely
19 √
20 √

Exercise S-116

1 better
2 tallest
3 less
4 longest
5 many
6 more quickly
7 as
8 more attractive
9 with
10 best
11 the most
12 more
13 less
14 better
15 faster
16 less
17 easier
18 to
19 wilder
20 worst

Exercise S−117

1 D	6 A
2 C	7 C
3 A	8 A
4 C	9 A
5 D	10 B

Exercise S−118

a–2	f–3
b–5	g–4
c–6	h–10
d–1	i–8
e–9	j-7

Exercise S-119

1 He asked where I lived.
2 Only once has he visited Texas.
3 It is not yet hot enough to swim.
4 Never had she seen so much rain in such a short time.
5 During the holidays, they plan to do something new every day.
6 My father taught me how to ride a horse at the age of six.
7 At parties, she always tells such humorous stories.
8 None of the cheese sandwiches on the dish were eaten.
9 She purchased a wool sweater at the department store.
10 Questions about how he was doing in school always bothered him.

Exercise S−120

No key

Exercise S−121

1 D	11 IND
2 IND	12 D
3 IND	13 IND
4 D	14 IND
5 IND	15 IND
6 IND	16 IND
7 D	17 D
8 IND	18 D
9 IND	19 IND
10 D	20 D

Exercise S−122

1 No one knows why the teacher was absent yesterday.
2 The instruction booklet explains what kind of batteries the toy needs.
3 Scientists cannot predict when the next earthquake will occur.
4 The professor informed the class when the test would be given.
5 She is old enough to go wherever she wants to go.
6 The reporters asked what time the president would arrive.
7 Sister Mystic can tell from the lines on your palm what your future will be.
8 The policeman asked him where he was going and why he was speeding.
9 The newspaper story doesn't state where the accident took place.
10 Zoo officials are puzzled about how the tiger got out of its cage.

Exercise S−123

1 √	whether . . . start	
2 √	whether . . . waited	
3 ×	if . . . evening	
4 √	if . . . regularly	
5 ×	if . . . graded	
6 √	if . . . time	
7 √	if . . . not	
8 ×	whether . . . washable	
9 √	if . . . found	
10 ×	if . . . dark	

Exercise S-124

1 Not only did they go, but they stayed until the end.
2 Only after her mother died did she know real loneliness.
3 At no time were the passengers in any danger.
4 Only once was John late to class.
5 Never has air pollution been as bad as it is now.
6 Seldom has his family seen him this angry.
7 Only after you have taken the placement test, can we tell you your level.
8 Scarcely had they sat down for dinner when the telephone rang.
9 Nowhere in the world is the weather so changeable as it is in Texas.
10 Only after it rains do the cacti in the desert bloom.

Exercise S-125

1 Were the truth known, that man would go to jail.
2 Had she passed the test, she would be smiling.
3 Had he gone to the doctor right away, he might have been alive today.
4 Were the old woman to get sick, she would not be able to call a doctor.
5 Should you see Fred, tell him to telephone me.
6 Were he not very sick, he would not be in the hospital.
7 Were it not important, my friend would not have asked me that favor.
8 Had he not gotten a raise, he would have resigned from the company.
9 Had they not borrowed some money, they could not have bought a new house.
10 Had he not been tired, he wouldn't have missed the party.

Exercise S-126

1 √
2 × was the boy
3 √
4 × are the gas stations
5 × was the book

6 × does the boy realize
7 √
8 √
9 √
10 × was her love

Exercise S-127

1 ...is a television set.
2 Not only did the police arrive,...
3 Scarcely had the injured man arrived...
4 Nowhere do children have...
5 So few were the woman's possessions...
6 ...will many people realize...
7 Seen leaving the convenience store were...
8 ...how much money each candidate was spending...
9 Never have foreign students come...
10 ...how quickly many species of cacti are becoming extinct.
11 Up came the flowers...
12 Little do they realize...
13 ...how Howard Hughes spent his final years.
14 Lying beside the road were...
15 There were several reasons...
16 √   21 √
17 ×   22 √
18 √   23 √
19 ×   24 ×
20 ×   25 ×

Exercise S-128

1 √	6 ×
2 ×	7 ×
3 ×	8 √
4 √	9 ×
5 ×	10 √

Exercise S-129

1 D	6 D
2 C	7 C
3 C	8 C
4 B	9 C
5 A	10 B

Exercise S-130

a–9	f–5
b–10	g–3
c–8	h–4
d–7	i–1
e–6	j–2

Exercise S-131

1 (energy)—their energy
2 (feeling happy)—happy
3 (interested)—interested in
4 (how they can get there)—how to get there
5 (to play)—playing
6 (To Speak)—Speaking
7 Not only was she pretty, but also she knew how to dress well.
8 (go)—go out
9 (Fred)—Fred's
10 (as fast)—as fast as

Exercise S-132

1 3–V	6 5–N
2 3–N	7 3–N
3 2–ADJ	8 2–ADJ
4 2–ADV	9 2–V
5 2–ADJ	10 4–N

Exercise S-133

1 a politician
2 accurate
3 alcohol
4 hungry
5 a glass of wine
6 poetry
7 three
8 equality
9 carefully
10 agreement

Exercise S-134

1 ×	6 ×
2 ×	7 √
3 ×	8 ×
4 √	9 ×
5 ×	10 √

Exercise S-135

1 SC	6 PHR
2 PHR	7 SC
3 SC	8 PHR
4 SC	9 SC
5 SC	10 SC

Exercise S-136

1 B	6 A
2 B	7 A
3 A	8 B
4 B	9 A
5 B	10 B

Exercise S-137

1 B	6 B
2 A	7 A
3 B	8 B
4 A	9 B
5 B	10 B

Exercise S-138

1 B
2 B
3 B
4 B
5 A

Exercise S-139

1 A	6 A
2 B	7 A
3 B	9 B
4 A	9 B
5 B	10 A

Exercise S-140

1 ×	11 √
2 ×	12 ×
3 ×	13 ×
4 ×	14 √
5 ×	15 √
6 ×	16 ×
7 ×	17 ×
8 ×	18 ×
9 ×	19 ×
10 ×	20 ×

Exercise S-141

1 C	6 D
2 D	7 A
3 A	8 D
4 C	9 B
5 D	10 D

Exercise S-142

a–5	f–6
b–2	g–10
c–7	h–1
d–3	i–4
e–8	j–9

Exercise S-143

(A) 3, 6	(F) 11, 16
(B) 1, 8	(G) 12, 19
(C) 2, 5	(H) 14, 17, 20
(D) 7, 10	(I) 13, 18
(E) 4, 9	(J) 15

Exercise S-144

more	less
exceed	decrease
enlarge	decline
inflate	deflate
surpass	reduce
outweigh	lower
augment	devalue
improve	regress
expand	relapse
overrate	deplete
ascend	diminish
accelerate	shrink
increase	undervalue

Exercise S-145

× = 1, 3, 4, 7, 9, 12, 13, 16, 17, 18, 20

Exercise S-146

1 The Kentucky rifle played an important part in helping early settlers get food.
2 The distant thunder was audible.
3 The Nandini is a popular shrub which was introduced into America from the Orient.
4 A room that is pink can soothe even the most violent prisoner.
5 Beginning with an investment of only ten thousand dollars, the two partners have increased their money by twenty thousand.
6 Extensive use of pesticides can kill pelicans.
7 Despite the repeal of the helmet law, not every motorcyclist has given up wearing a helmet.

8 Almost simultaneously, residents in several parts of the city were experiencing severe flooding.
9 In the 1960's, Students all over the country were discussing the war and protesting against it.
10 Although the short report was well written and documented, it failed to convince the committee to vote against the project.
11 There are several important reasons for the nation to invest money in renewable energy sources.
12 The only quick way to rid a yard of fleas is to spray all vegetation thoroughly.
13 Since squashbugs can kill young plants almost overnight, it is very important to check the garden daily.
14 The city is quite fortunate to have two daily newspapers that provide both local and national coverage.
15 A male tiger may outweigh a female by seventy to one hundred pounds.
16 A student is less likely to fail an examination if he knows exactly what topics will be tested.
17 The reason one should read every day is to improve one's speed and comprehension.
18 The dog was purchased to guard the house and yard while the owners were away.
19 The issues that divided the States and brought about the Civil War were not easily resolved.
20 A hot iron can scorch delicate fabrics quickly.

Exercise S–147

1 A	6 B
2 B	7 C
3 D	8 B
4 C	9 B
5 D	10 D

Exercise S–148

a–8	f–3
b–5	g–2
c–6	h–1
d–10	i–4
e–7	j–9

Exercise S–149

two	three
either	most
both	largest
less	least
inferior	among
neither	worst
superior	none
better	best
former	all
more	
between	
latter	
worse	

Exercise S–150

1 A	6 A
2 A	7 A
3 A	8 B
4 B	9 A
5 A	10 B

Exercise S–151

1 sit, sat, sat, sitting	7 raised	13 lain
2 set, set, set, setting	8 risen	14 laid
3 lie, lay, lain, lying	9 rose	15 laid
4 lay, laid, laid, laying	10 sat	16 lying
5 rise, rose, risen, rising	11 set	
6 raise, raised, raised, raising	12 set	

Exercise S–152

1	A–×	(risen)	11	P–×	(laid)
2	A–√		12	A–×	(rise)
3	A–×	(lain)	13	A–√	
4	A–×	(setting)	14	P–×	(set)
5	P–√		15	A–×	(sitting)
6	A–√		16	P–√	
7	P–×	(raised)	17	P–√	
8	A–√		18	P–×	(raised)
9	A–√		19	P–√	
10	P–√		20	A–×	(lay)

Exercise S–153

1 C	6 B
2 D	7 A
3 B	8 C
4 A	9 D
5 A	10 D

Exercise S–154

take	make	do
your time	a mistake	housework
a trip	a comparison	a favor
medicine	a suggestion	an experiment
(money)	arrangements	your best
an airplane	a proposal	a good job
(a bet)	an appointment	homework
a chance	friends	exercises
a turn	advances	a project
	(a trip)	research
	a speech	
	an effort	
	(medicine)	
	money	
	(an airplane)	
	a bet	
	a promise	
	progress	
	(a turn)	
	a deposit	
	a recommendation	
	a reservation	

Exercise S–155

1 A	6 A
2 B	7 B
3 A	8 A
4 A	9 A
5 B	10 B

Exercise S–156

a	an
university	orange
union	hour
home	honest person
uniform	umpire
hurricane	honorary degree
one-story house	honor
unit	umbrella
once-familiar face	herb
	only child
	owner

96

Exercise S—157

1	a	11	a
2	an	12	an
3	an	13	a
4	a	14	an
5	a	15	a
6	an	16	an
7	a	17	a
8	an	18	an
9	a	19	an
10	an	20	a

Exercise S-158

count	non-count
acids	companionship
arrivals	information
techniques	furniture
decisions	exhaustion
withdrawals	evaporation
challenges	oxygen
electrons	aluminum
substances	electricity
organisms	moisture
ages	lumber
waves	architecture
enthusiasts	accounting

Exercise S-159

count	both	non-count
few	any	little
several	the	amount
a/an	some	less
both	all	much
each/every		
many		
one/two/three		
neither of/either of		
quantity		
fewer		

Exercise S—160

1	B	6	B
2	A	7	A
3	B	8	A
4	A	9	A
5	A	10	B

Exercise S—161

$\sqrt{} = 2, 8, 17$

Exercise S-162

No key

Exercise S-163

1	B	6	B
2	C	7	B
3	A	8	D
4	A	9	D
5	D	10	D

Key for Section 3:
Reading Comprehension and Vocabulary

Exercise R–1
No key

Exercise R–2
2 special: unusual/common
3 concern: worried/nonchalant
4 cope with: contend with/ignore
5 please: attractive/disagreeable
6 penalty: disadvantage/reward
7 benefit: advantage/drawback
8 substance: considerable/inconsequential

Exercise R–3

2 poultry	**rooster**	hen	chick
3 horses	stallion	**mare**	colt/foal
4 dogs	dog	bitch	**puppy**
5 **geese**	gander	goose	gosling
6 deer	**buck**	doe	fawn
7 bears	bear	**bear**	cub
8 ducks	drake	duck	**duckling**
9 **lions**	lion	lioness	cub
10 cats	**tom cat**	cat	kitten

Exercise R–4

kitchen	**bedroom**	**bathroom**	**living room**
refrigerator	dresser	tub	couch
stove	chest of drawers	toilet	recliner
chopping block	night stand	medicine cabinet	ottoman

dining room	**patio**	**office**	
dining table	lawn chair	swivel chair	
buffet	barbeque grill	desk	
china cabinet	hammock	filing cabinet	

Exercise R–5
No key

Exercise R–6

1 C		6 C	
2 C		7 A	
3 A		8 D	
4 C		9 B	
5 B		10 B	

Exercise R–7

1 B		6 D	
2 A		7 B	
3 D		8 C	
4 C		9 C	
5 A		10 A	

Exercise R–8

1 B		6 C	
2 D		7 B	
3 A		8 D	
4 A		9 C	
5 B		10 A	

Exercise R—9

1 The administration
2 Professor Elkins
3 Liza Minelli
4 the woman . . . the ship
5 Leonard
6 a spokesman for the film company
7 Michael Cimino
8 small bankers
9 all foreign investors
10 The basketball team

Exercise R—10

1 Hemingway
2 the man with the limp
3 the playwright
4 Mrs. Jones
5 the woman
6 the general's daughter
7 the Shepherds
8 patients
9 stutterers
10 insects of all kinds

Exercise R—11

1 the former home of John D. Spreckels
2 San Diego
3 his first bicycle
4 the music teacher
5 Elizabeth Monroe
6 Sterne
7 Ken Berdeen
8 the Bushmen
9 Shakespeare's plays
10 The defendants

Exercise R—12

1 Jean—cakes
2 Marion Rice—methods
3 Sally—paintings
4 Van Cliburn—concert careers
5 Pierre Cardin—restaurant
6 Bill—article
7 the members of the boys' club—float
8 David and Roxanna—apartment
9 The English—archers
10 John—recipes

Exercise R—13

1 a grant of two million dollars
2 a new project
3 the need for less sleep
4 drink
5 drunkenness
6 the Bahamas
7 physical disorders
8 a Mercedes and a condominium
9 two reasons
10 his favourite pastimes
11 problems with balance
12 a flag and a national anthem
13 Fuchsia and mauve
14 1963 to 1968
15 signs of aging

Exercise R—14

1 four minutes
2 to follow their original line
3 a gold watch
4 Many educators . . . a teacher.
5 take out the boy's appendix.
6 the Thunderbird
7 fund . . . Indies.
8 Albert Einstein . . . a child.
9 Waterloo
10 John F. Kennedy . . . November 22, 1963.
11 The treasurer . . . embezzlement.
12 raw egg yolk—anchovies
13 wrecked three cars
14 covered his eyes—moaned softly
15 best-sellers
16 five restaurants
17 several Spanish courses
18 a 25 percent wage increase—enforcement . . . regulations.
19 He drank and ate to excess
20 he had taken lessons . . . Baseball.

Exercise R–15

1 clocks
2 shows
3 proposals
4 lithographs
5 questions
6 applications
7 archeological sites
8 alternatives
9 Los Angeles
10 John Glenn's orbital journey
11 basic research
12 acrobats

Exercise R–16

1.1 this
2 these
3 Those
4 that

2.1 they
2 it
3 its
4 them

3.1 these
2 those
3 hers
4 her
5 she
6 its

4.1 he
2 his
3 it
4 him
5 their
6 theirs

5.1 One
2 his
3 he
4 ones
5 the latter's
6 the former's

6.1 theirs
2 his
3 them
4 its
5 him
6 this
7 that

7.1 her
2 she
3 them
4 their
5 they
6 theirs
7 hers

8.1 they
2 their
3 it
4 This
5 these

9.1 These
2 His
3 her
4 those
5 This
6 her

10.1 One
2 this
3 them
4 the former
5 the latter
6 ones

Exercise R–17

1.1 streams
2 They
3 woods
4 them
5 miles
6 it

2.1 it
2 operetta
3 performance
4 the authors'
5 there
6 These
7 their

3.1 they
2 thousand
3 million
4 these
5 deaths
6 injuries
7 those

4.1 prejudices
2 it
3 advantages
4 these
5 abundance
6 This
7 rates

5.1 physicist
2 he
3 them
4 This
5 novelist
6 his
7 novel
8 Gell—Mann's
9 discovery
10 physics

6.1 they
  2 value
  3 86.3
  4 which
  5 country
  6 state
  7 flowers
  8 300
  9 These

7.1 it
  2 earth
  3 ice
  4 this
  5 planet's
  6 fresh water
  7 oceans
  8 their

8.1 inhabitants
  2 their
  3 waters
  4 irrigation projects
  5 This
  6 dams
  7 one
  8 river
  9 people
  10 it
  11 its
  12 these

9.1 understandings
  2 life
  3 behavior
  4 he
  5 human beings
  6 their

10.1 prices
  2 rates
  3 150,000
  4 house
  5 suburbs
  6 residences
  7 fashionable part
  8 1,000,000
  9 This
  10 it
  11 those
  12 that

Exercise R–18

1.1 The pyramids . . . the Nile
  2 the pyramids/royal tombs
  3 the pyramid/royal tomb
  4 the one that housed the pharaoh Khufu/Cheops

2.1 King Edward III
  2 the title of Duke of Cornwall
  3 Duke of Cornwall

3.1 The streets of Manhattan
  2 The streets of Manhattan
  3 laws regulating . . . traffic
  4 bicycle messengers
  5 bicycle messengers
  6 bicycle messengers

4.1 Saturn's rings
  2 forces
  3 sheet of particles
  4 sheet of particles
  5 sheet of particles—denser at certain spots
  6 nearby particles
  7 Voyager 2

5.1 oil company
  2 one of . . . vessels
  3 typical oil exploration ship
  4 typical oil exploration ship
  5 raw data
  6 the crew
  7 make preliminary analyses . . . closer look
  8 invisible spot . . . oil

6.1 the engineers
   2 their latest model
   3 the engineers
   4 what they did not change
   5 their latest model
   6 their latest model

7.1 The American Museum of Natural History
   2 four years
   3 the decades archeologists have spent digging for and studying gold artifacts
   4 prehistoric Indians
   5 500 pieces of ancient gold from Colombia/gold artifacts

8.1 the Wisconsin
   2 the Wisconsin
   3 its winding course to the Mississippi
   4 the Wisconsin
   5 the Wisconsin
   6 Wisconsinites
   7 Wisconsinites
   8 Their fertile farmlands

9.1 The person sits up in bed suddenly, talks incoherently . . . But no external
    danger is present.
   2 The person
   3 The person
   4 It happens early . . . But no external danger is present.
   5 this episode
   6 one of two distinct phenomena
   7 one of two distinct phenomena

10.1 stalking followed by an "all out" chase.
    2 the fox
    3 a hare/its prey
    4 the fox
    5 the hare
    6 When it closes in . . . in the leg.
    7 the hare
    8 the hare
    9 the fox/the predator
    10 the predator gets a hold on its quarry
    11 the hare
    12 the fox
    13 the hare/its victim.

Exercise R–19

1 C	6 B
2 B	7 C
3 D	8 A
4 D	9 A
5 A	10 D

Exercise R–20

1 B	6 C	11 B	16 C
2 A	7 C	12 D	17 A
3 D	8 B	13 A	18 D
4 B	9 D	14 A	19 A
5 B	10 B	15 D	20 C

Exercise R–21

1 C	6 D
2 D	7 A
3 B	8 D
4 C	9 D
5 B	10 B

Exercise R–22

1 B	6 D
2 D	7 C
3 D	8 D
4 C	9 A
5 A	10 B

Exercise R–23

1 B	6 A
2 B	7 A
3 A	8 B
4 B	9 A
5 A	10 A

Exercise R–24, Part A

1 F	6 A
2 F	7 F
3 A	8 F
4 F	9 A
5 A	10 F

Exercise R–24, Part B

1 A	6 A
2 F	7 F
3 A	8 A
4 F	9 F
5 A	10 A

Exercise R–25

1 B	6 C
2 C	7 B
3 A	8 B
4 B	9 C
5 C	10 B

Exercise R–26

1.1$\sqrt{}$–2B–3A–4C
2.1C–2A–3B–4$\sqrt{}$
3.1C–2B–3$\sqrt{}$–4A
4.1A–2$\sqrt{}$–3B–4C
5.1C–2B–3A–4$\sqrt{}$

Exercise R–27

1 H	6 G
2 B	7 I
3 J	8 E
4 D	9 A
5 C	10 F

Exercise R–28

1 D	6 H
2 J	7 G
3 A	8 C
4 F	9 E
5 I	10 B

Exercise R–29

1 H	5 G
2 D	6 A
3 F	7 E
4 B	8 C

Exercise R–30

1 E	5 C
2 A	6 H
3 D	7 F
4 G	

Exercise R–31

1 D	5 E
2 B	6 G
3 F	7 A
4 H	8 C

Exercise R–32

1 D	6 A
2 J	7 I
3 E	8 F
4 G	9 H
5 B	10 C

Exercise R–33

1 E	6 G
2 J	7 F
3 H	8 C
4 B	9 I
5 D	10 A

Exercise R–34

1	E	6	H
2	A	7	D
3	F	8	J
4	B	9	G
5	I	10	C

Exercise R–35

1	B	5	H
2	D	6	C
3	F	7	G
4	E	8	A

Exercise R–36

1	E	6	G
2	A	7	B
3	D	8	J
4	F	9	C
5	I	10	H

Exercise R–37

1	D
2	C
3	B
4	A
5	B

Exercise R–38

1	A	6	C
2	C	7	B
3	A	8	D
4	D	9	C
5	B	10	B

Exercise R–39

1	B, D	6	A, B
2	B, D	7	B, C
3	A, C	8	B, C
4	A, C, D	9	B, C
5	D	10	B, C

Exercise R–40

1	A, C	6	A, B
2	B, D	7	A, C
3	A, B	8	A, B, C
4	B	9	A, C, D
5	B, C	10	A, B

Exercise R–41

2	B	6	B
3	C	7	A
4	A	8	C
5	B	9	A
		10	C

Exercise R–42

1	A	6	B
2	C	7	C
3	C	8	B
4	B	9	A
5	A	10	C

Exercise R–43

1	C	6	A
2	A	7	C
3	C	8	B
4	B	9	C
5	C	10	B

Exercise R–44

1	A	6	A	11	C	16	B
2	D	7	C	12	D	17	C
3	B	8	C	13	C	18	A
4	C	9	B	14	B	19	B
5	D	10	D	15	D	20	D

Exercise R–45

1	C	6	A
2	D	7	B
3	C	8	A
4	C	9	D
5	D	10	C

Exercise R–46

1	B	6	C
2	B	7	A
3	C	8	A
4	B	9	B
5	A	10	C

Exercise R–47

1	B
2	D
3	A
4	C
5	C

Exercise R–48

1 A	6 D
2 C	7 B
3 B	8 A
4 C	9 A
5 C	10 D

Exercise R–49

1 D	6 A
2 C	7 C
3 B	8 D
4 B	9 A
5 A	10 A

Exercise R–50

1 B	4 A
2 C	5 D
3 E	6 F

Exercise R–51

1 F	4 A
2 D	5 C
3 E	6 B

Exercise R–52

1 C	4 A
2 D	5 B
3 F	6 E

Exercise R–53

1 although
2 despite
3 Because of
4 If
5 Unless
6 however
7 Furthermore
8 Since

Exercise R–54

1 Nevertheless
2 consequently
3 Otherwise
4 while
5 unless
6 so that
7 in addition
8 because
9 For all that
10 because of

Exercise R–55

1 Even though
2 it
3 moreover
4 the bicycle
5 its
6 whereas
7 matter
8 no matter how
9 by contrast
10 In fact
11 in spite of
12 so

Exercise R–56

1 it
2 food
3 Since
4 and
5 however
6 but
7 their
8 wheat's
9 them
10 wheat production
11 scientists
12 wild relatives

Exercise R–57

1 cats
2 The cats
3 then
4 their
5 the brain cells
6 those
7 sleep
8 because
9 However
10 brain cells
11 These
12 the sleep
13 Dreams
14 The dreams
15 them

Exercise R–58

1 and by July 4
2 through 1976
3 throughout 1976
4 on about July 4, 1976
5 from 1976 on

Exercise R–59

1 for over four years
2 over four years
3 in the latter four years
4 during the four years
5 Until four years ago

Exercise R–60

1 in ten years' time
2 over the last ten years of this century
3 for the last ten years
4 in the last ten years of the
   nineteenth century
5 ten years ago today

Exercise R–61

1 six months ago
2 Not until six months later
3 since six months ago
4 over the coming six months
5 Until six months ago

Exercise R–62

1 A		6 C	
2 C		7 A	
3 B		8 B	
4 A		9 A	
5 B		10 B	

Exercise R–63

1 −		6 +	
2 +		7 −	
3 −		8 −	
4 +		9 −	
5 +		10 +	

Exercise R–64

1 +

Sandals are much\far more comfortable than high-heeled shoes.

2 −

Men's bodies have much\far more muscle than women's bodies.

3 +

Fruit juice has more calories than soda water.

4 +

Rembrandt is much\far more famous than Delacroix.

5 +

Gigli sang much\far more sweetly than Caruso.

6 −

Polenz played the part more spectacularly than Williams.

7 −

Soccer offers more continuous action than football.

8 +

Chess requires more concentration than checkers.

9 −

Los Angeles has far more Mexican inhabitants than most Mexican state capitals.

10 +

English derives from far more different roots than other languages.

Exercise R–65

1	–	6	+
2	–	7	+
3	+	8	=
4	=	9	–
5	+	10	+

Exercise R–66

1 the sudden increase in demand
2 Many school programs underrate children's intelligence
3 receiving a large advance for a book about newspaper corruption
4 an increased understanding of the nature of animal suffering by the community
5 very specific demands on the person's time
6 his new-found popularity
7 the sheer enjoyment they get from the activity itself
8 over-enthusiastic diversification
9 The post office's concern at its declining reputation for reliability
10 A yearning for higher soccer scores
11 such apparently marginal features as the type of clothes they wear
12 both her parents had been doctors
13 his family's precarious financial state and his wife's failing health
14 the dissatisfaction of many women's organizations with earlier findings
15 Cable News Network proved the existence of a surprisingly large 2 to 5 a.m. television audience

Exercise R–67

1	A	6	A	11	B
2	B	7	A	12	A
3	B	8	B	13	A
4	A	9	B	14	B
5	B	10	A	15	B

Exercise R–68

1	F	6	T
2	T	7	T
3	T	8	F
4	F	9	F
5	T	10	T

Exercise R–69

	(A)	(B)	(C)	(D)
1	F	T	T	T
2	T	T	T	F
3	F	T	T	T

Exercise R–70

(1) 2, 4, 7
(2) 5, 1
(3) 3
(4) 6

Exercise R–71

1 T
2 F: Two slices of whole wheat bread are allowed each day.
3 F: Liquor should be replaced by iced tea without sugar or soda water with lime or lemon.
4 F: Steamed potatoes without butter or sauces are recommended as part of the diet.
5 T
6 T
7 F: No sauces should be consumed except tomato ketchup with no added sugar.
8 T
9 T
10 F: The suggested desserts are healthy and low in fat.

Exercise R–72

1 F: The vacancies at East End Mall will be filled by stores which fit the mall's image.
2 T
3 F: East End Mall became popular immediately.
4 F: East End Mall is the only shopping center in the area which provides free child care.
5 T
6 F: East End Mall is better than Westgate in terms of availability of movie entertainment.
7 T
8 T
9 T
10 F: The trees and shrubbery surrounding the mall are intended to grow in order to camouflage the main buildings and parking lot.

Exercise R–73

1 T
2 F: Efforts made by the religious community initiated the recent rise in Klondyke Park's respectability.
3 T
4 F: People often work or read in the park, especially on weekdays.
5 F: Motorized vehicles are prohibited from the park and the playing of radios is discouraged.
6 F: Most dogs in the park are well-supervised by their owners.
7 T
8 F: Eating is allowed in grassy picnic areas.
9 F: Scout troops meet regularly in the larger, open spaces of Klondyke Park.
10 T

Exercise R–74

1 F: The aim of *Expressing Yourself in English* is to approach learning English in a way which varies slightly from the traditional.
2 T
3 T
4 F: The book contains twenty-four illustrated readings.
5 F: Teachers are instructed to answer the students' questions about reading comprehension only after the students have worked through the exercises on their own.
6 T
7 T
8 F: The verb *to be* is not introduced until Unit 3 of this text.
9 T
10 F: The workbook will be published later this year.

Exercise R–75

1 T
2 T
3 F: The college no longer offers degrees in oriental languages.
4 F: The college's sports program excludes football.
5 F: McGaffic College has an all-male student population.
6 T
7 T

8 T

9 F: The chemistry department is the only science department not to have had representatives win awards in national science competitions.

10 F: McGaffic College welcomes applications from young men throughout the country.

Exercise R—76

1 A	6 C
2 C	7 B
3 B	8 B
4 D	9 A
5 B	10 B

Key for Section 4:
The Test of Written English (TWE)

Exercise W—1

1 The use of nuclear energy to generate electricity: for and against.
2 A Say which s/he would favor for her/his country.
  B Reasons for A.

Exercise W—2

1 For
2 A Nuclear energy to produce electricity is cheaper.
  B Other ways use up non-renewable energy sources.
  C Countries without non-nuclear energy sources have to depend on an unreliable supply of energy from other countries.
3 B
4 Main idea: Nuclear energy production is not safe.
  A Immediate results of an accident — devastating.
  B Long-term results — insidious.
  C Accidents do happen, e.g. Three-Mile-Island and Chernobyl.
5 Sentence 1: Say which side you would favor for your country.
  Sentences 2—5: Give reasons for your answer.

Exercise W—4

Step 1 A The use of nuclear energy to generate electricity: for and against.
         C Give reasons for her/his answer (i.e. her/his opinion on what is best for her/his country).

Step 2 **For**: B Doesn't use up finite resources, e.g. coal and oil.
         Against: A Nuclear accidents have terrible immediate results.
                          C 1 Three-Mile-Island (USA).
                              2 Chernobyl (USSR).

Step 3 A <u>Against</u> using nuclear energy to produce electricity.

   B Paragraph 2. To write a reasonable essay, you must present logical arguments for *both* sides of the issue. The writer has presented good arguments in favor of nuclear energy in Paragraph 1 and then followed these with even stronger arguments, in her/his opinion, against nuclear energy. Readers tend to expect the strongest arguments last; the writer has followed the old maxim: "Save the best 'til last".

Step 4 A **Paragraph 1**: Proponents of using nuclear energy to produce electricity usually put forward three fundamental arguments, two of them economic and the third political.
   Paragraph 2: The most common argument against the use of nuclear energy is based on safety.

   B In Paragraph 1, the topic sentence tells the reader that this paragraph contains the arguments of proponents of nuclear energy. More specifically, the sentence says the reader will find "three fundamental arguments, two of them economic and the third political". The paragraph goes on to give these arguments.

   The topic sentence in Paragraph 2 tells the reader that this paragraph will focus on the biggest argument against nuclear energy: safety. The remainder of the paragraph explains why the question of safety alone makes a strong case against nuclear energy.

Step 5 Compare the information in the simple outline in Step 2 above with Paragraphs 1 and 2. In each, the writer has written complete sentences that are related to each other and to the topic sentence. The writer has made it easy for the reader to follow her/his argument.

Step 6 A <u>Against</u> using nuclear energy to produce electricity.
   B 1 Ample supplies of oil and hydroelectric energy.
      2 No guarantee of safety.
      3 Better uses for the money.

Step 7 B When presenting your arguments, as the writer has done in Paragraphs 1 and 2, you should present them as facts and therefore avoid personal pronouns. *I*, *my*, and *we* belong in paragraphs where opinion is appropriate. Since the question asks for the writer's opinion, it *is* appropriate to use these personal pronouns in the paragraph where s/he states a personal opinion.

Exercise W—13

1 The changing trends in family expenditure in the United States as indicated by the two graphs.
2 Food, Savings, Education
3 Rent, Leisure, Household appliances
4 Transportation

Exercise W—15

1 B
   The writer thinks that the changes in the minor expenditures reflect some important changes that have occurred.

2 35%—25%; 28%—35%
   A In general, these are the two most important necessities. The writer summarizes the changes in expenditure that have taken place.

110

B The writer interprets the trends to show that people may be eating more sensibly and living in better houses. But note that the total for the two items remained at about three-fifths of family expenditure.

3 In 1950, Food + Rent = 63%. In 1980, Food + Rent = 60%. A difference of 3%. In 1950, Household appliances = 5% and in 1980 = 8%. A difference of 3%. Since household appliances are related to food preparation and to other household needs, the writer put the three categories together, making the 3% difference in Food + Rent between 1950 and 1980 disappear.

These percentages are significant to the writer in that in both 1950 and 1980, the total expenditure on food, rent, household appliances and transportation came to seventy-eight percent. The remaining twenty-two percent spent on savings, education and leisure represents the "significant trends" the writer discusses in Paragraphs 4 and 5.

4 Leisure had the greatest proportional increase of any category between 1950 and 1980, and since we have seen that food, rent, household appliances and transportation as a group showed no change, the money for extra leisure activities came from the other two categories: education and savings.

5 The writer thinks that the trends are dangerous because the categories in which significant change have occurred reflect people's concern for immediate satisfaction and disregard for the future.

I think the writer would advise these families to re-examine their priorities and to consider their responsibility for their children's and their society's future.

Key for Section 5: Practice Tests I and II
Practice Test I

Section 1: Listening Comprehension

1 C 2 A 3 B 4 D 5 A 6 C 7 B 8 C 9 B 10 A 11 D 12 B 13 D
14 C 15 A 16 D 17 D 18 A 19 C 20 B

21 D 22 A 23 D 24 B 25 C 26 C 27 A 28 B 29 D 30 C 31 C 32 D
33 A 34 B 35 B

36 B 37 A 38 D 39 C 40 D 41 C 42 B 43 A 44 B 45 D 46 A 47 C
48 A 49 D 50 C

Section 2: Structure and Written Expression

1 A 2 D 3 D 4 B 5 C 6 A 7 C 8 B 9 D 10 A 11 C 12 D 13 D
14 A 15 B

16 D 17 D 18 B 19 D 20 A 21 C 22 D 23 A 24 B 25 B 26 A 27 B
28 C 29 D 30 C 31 B 32 A 33 C 34 C 35 C 36 A 37 D 38 C
39 C 40 D

Section 3: Reading Comprehension and Vocabulary

1 D 2 A 3 D 4 B 5 C 6 A 7 C 8 D 9 B 10 C 11 A 12 D 13 C
14 B 15 A 16 D 17 B 18 C 19 D 20 B 21 C 22 B 23 C 24 A 25 D
26 A 27 C 28 D 29 B 30 A

31 A 32 D 33 C 34 B 35 C 36 D 37 D 38 D 39 A 40 C 41 B 42 A
43 B 44 D 45 A 46 C 47 D 48 C 49 B 50 D 51 A 52 C 53 B 54 B
55 D 56 B 57 A 58 C 59 A 60 B

Practice Test II

Section 1: Listening Comprehension

1 D 2 D 3 A 4 C 5 B 6 C 7 A 8 D 9 B 10 C 11 D 12 A 13 B
14 C 15 B 16 A 17 A 18 D 19 B 20 C

21 A 22 C 23 D 24 B 25 C 26 A 27 C 28 D 29 B 30 B 31 A 32 A
33 B 34 D 35 C

36 D 37 A 38 D 39 C 40 C 41 B 42 B 43 A 44 D 45 C 46 B 47 A
48 A 49 D 50 C

Section 2: Structure and Written Expression

1 B 2 C 3 A 4 D 5 B 6 C 7 D 8 A 9 C 10 B 11 C 12 A 13 C
14 A 15 D

16 D 17 D 18 B 19 C 20 C 21 B 22 A 23 C 24 A 25 B 26 C 27 D
28 A 29 D 30 B 31 C 32 A 33 B 34 C 35 D 36 B 37 A 38 C 39 D
40 B

Section 3: Reading Comprehension and Vocabulary

1 B 2 C 3 D 4 A 5 C 6 B 7 A 8 B 9 D 10 C 11 D 12 A
13 C 14 B 15 D 16 A 17 B 18 A 19 D 20 A 21 C 22 D 23 B 24 C
25 D 26 A 27 B 28 D 29 A 30 C

31 C 32 C 33 A 34 B 35 D 36 A 37 B 38 D 39 B 40 A 41 B 42 D
43 C 44 A 45 C 46 D 47 C 48 A 49 B 50 B 51 D 52 B 53 A 54 D
55 C 56 B 57 C 58 D 59 C 60 A

TOEFL Answer Sheet

Name

Completely blacken the oval that corresponds to the answer you have chosen.
Erase all other marks. This is the correct way to make your answer: (A) (B) ● (D)

SECTION 1

SECTION 2

SECTION 3

Thomas Nelson and Sons Ltd
Nelson House   Mayfield Road
Walton-on-Thames   Surrey
KT12 5PL   UK

51 York Place
Edinburgh EH1 3JD   UK

Thomas Nelson (Hong Kong) Ltd
Toppan Building 10/F
22A Westlands Road
Quarry Bay   Hong Kong

© Carol King and Nancy Stanley 1983,
1989

Original edition first published by
Thomas Nelson and Sons Ltd 1983

This edition first published by
Thomas Nelson and Sons Ltd 1989

ISBN 0−17−555730−6 2nd edition
(ISBN 0−17−555453−6 1st edition)
NPN 9 8 7 6 5 4 3

Printed in Hong Kong